The Beatles' England

The Beatles' England

there are places I'll remember

by David Bacon and Norman Maslov

910 Press
San Francisco

The Beatles' England
A 910 Press Book
PO Box 22361
San Francisco, Ca. 94122

Designed by Brenn Lea Pearson
Cover photograph of the Beatles by Dezo Hoffman/Rex Features
Handtinting by Wendy Schwartz

Library of Congress Catalog Card Number: 81-82555
ISBN: 0-9606736-0-1 Clothbound
        0-9606736-1-X Softcover

10 9 8 7 6 5 4 3 2 1

Printed in Japan by Dai Nippon Co., Ltd.

Contents

London *(continued)*

Liverpool 68

Daytripping

Introduction

A few years ago we made our first trip to England, a pilgrimage that all dedicated Beatles fans should attempt to make. We did our homework beforehand, writing down a list of places that we wanted to visit, and addresses if we could find them. Savile Row, Abbey Road and 7 Cavendish were easy to find, but some of the more obscure places were almost impossible. We did our best and what we saw amazed us. We thought we knew it all, but after visiting these sites a whole new dimension of understanding became clearer to us. For example, we didn't realize how close NEMS was to the Cavern Club (98 steps), or why the businesses of Savile Row would object to a rooftop concert, or what a radically different neighborhood Pete Best lived in compared to the other Beatles, or the full splendor of Friar Park.

Since that first visit, we have made several return journeys to England, adding to our own experiences and knowledge, and bringing about a better understanding of the beast! We found the soul that surrounded the Beatles and touched the walls from where they came (with the temptation to take pieces of the walls home with us).

This is when the idea hit us for compiling a photo-book that would serve both as an in-hand guide for Beatles-tourists, as well as an illustrated biography using places rather than time as the framework.

The Beatles' England is divided into three major sections: *London, Liverpool* and *Daytripping* (a section including those places outside of London and Liverpool). We have included what we feel are the most important and interesting sites throughout the Beatles' England.

Please remember that many of these places are now the homes and businesses of non-Beatle people, so be courteous regarding their property and privacy. Beatles fans will make this pilgrimage for generations to come. These places we'll remember.

David Bacon and Norman Maslov—1981

9

There are places I'll remember
all my life, though some have changed.
Some forever, not for better,
some have gone and some remain.
All these places had their moments
with lovers and friends I still can recall,
Some are dead and some are living,
In my life I've loved them all.

John Lennon and Paul McCartney

Oxford Street, London

London

An old city   dark with fog   black taxis on narrow streets
red buses stacked up   crowded West End sidewalks   tube
stop congestion   buildings with scaffolding: to let
Royal Parks surrounding familiar Palaces   Buckingham
Westminster   Big Ben   the Tower Bridge crossing the Thames
BBC changing channels   record shops and cinemas
empty Indian restaurants   greasy fish and chips   dark Soho Pubs
British Museum   the Tate   National Portrait Gallery
Covent Gardens   Trafalgar Square   Oxford Street   Abbey Road.

London

Abbey Road Crosswalk

Intersection of Abbey Road and Grove End Road

Riddle: Why did the Beatles cross the road?

Answer: To take an album cover photograph.

Next to *Sgt. Pepper's Lonely Hearts Club Band*, the LP cover of the Beatles' *Abbey Road* became their most famous and familiar. It brought attention to an otherwise relatively

unknown London intersection, making it a mecca for Beatles fans from all over the world.

As a Beatles fan, the first place you must go to when you arrive in London is Abbey Road. Nowhere else first! It's a rule...a must! Forget about Buckingham Palace, or Big Ben or even your hotel. Abbey Road is first. It is the Beatles fan's Xanadu! After all, in Rome, Catholics first visit the Vatican, and Jews in Jerusalem go to the Wailing Wall and manic

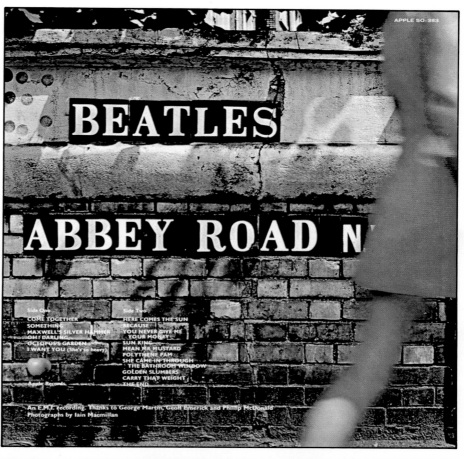

APPLE SO-383

BEATLES
ABBEY ROAD N

Side One
COME TOGETHER
SOMETHING
MAXWELL'S SILVER HAMMER
OH! DARLING
OCTOPUS'S GARDEN
I WANT YOU (She's so heavy)

Side Two
HERE COMES THE SUN
BECAUSE
YOU NEVER GIVE ME
  YOUR MONEY
SUN KING
MEAN MR MUSTARD
POLYTHENE PAM
SHE CAME IN THROUGH
  THE BATHROOM WINDOW
GOLDEN SLUMBERS
CARRY THAT WEIGHT
THE END

Apple Records

An E.M.I. recording. Thanks to George Martin, Geoff Emerick and Philip McDonald
Photographs by Iain Macmillan

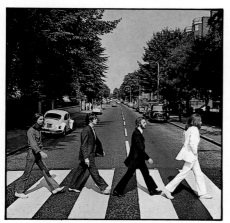

Abbey Road Crosswalk
(continued)

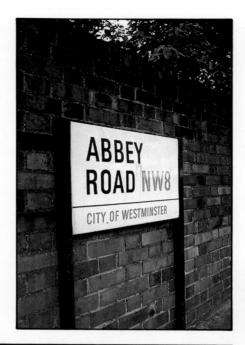

depressives in San Francisco head straight for the Golden Gate Bridge. But you, the true Beatlemaniac, must go straight to the Abbey Road crosswalk. Nowhere else is more sacred.

When you arrive at the crosswalk which is at the intersection of Abbey Road and Grove End Road, stop and stand there for a moment. Look around at the buildings, smell the air and listen to everything around you. Feel the vibrations of the asphalt below your feet. Become the sidewalk. You have arrived! Be careful when kissing the ground though, traffic is coming at you regularly and rapidly. ∎

The Beatles posed at the crosswalk at 10:00 am on August 8, 1969. Breaking their pattern of afternoon sessions for the Abbey Road *LP, they arrived in the morning for the photo session to elude the usual waiting fans.*

Abbey Road Studios (EMI)
3 Abbey Road

EMI's recording studio at 3 Abbey Road is the place where most of the Beatles' records were created. As they say, "if the walls had ears."

The walls of EMI studios first heard the Beatles' music on June 6, 1962, when the band auditioned for Parlaphone Records' head of artist-and-repertoire, George Martin. The Beatles were put under contract.

On September 11 they recorded their first single, *Love Me Do*, backed with *P.S. I Love You* in Studio Number Two. Between the time of the audition and their first session, drummer Pete Best had an accident; he fell out of favor with the rest of the group. Ringo Starr then became the luckiest man in the world when he wisely left Rory Storm and the Hurricanes to join the Beatles.

Meanwhile, George Martin, being the conservative, tie-wearing sort, was unsure of Ringo's ability on the drums, so he hired Andy White, a studio drummer, to sit in on the session. Ringo and Andy traded off during a number of takes. The single that was first released featured Ringo on drums, but the version of *Love Me Do* that was later issued on the *Please, Please Me* album had Andy on drums and Ringo on tambourine.

Love Me Do became a mediocre national hit. George Martin wanted the Beatles to record *How Do You Do It* written by Mitch Murray for their next single. A sure hit he thought. But the Beatles didn't like it and wanted to release one of their own compositions. So the song, *Please, Please Me* a rejected B-side of their

Abbey Road Studios
(continued)

first single, was rearranged and re-recorded, giving the Beatles their first number-one hit.

On February 11, 1963, the Beatles with George Martin once again entered Studio Number Two at 10:30 in the morning and recorded and mixed their entire first album on EMI's antique two-track recorder. As an afterthought, the song *Twist and Shout* was recorded at the very end of the session. John Lennon's voice was almost gone, and the song had to be screamed live, in one take.

After the popularity of the debut album, *Please, Please Me*, the Beatles were given more recording time at EMI studios. And with each subse-quent release, they had a bigger hit. EMI eventually gave them free reign of the studio, allowing experimentation to begin. By 1966, as touring ended, EMI became more than just a studio for the Beatles. It became virtually the only place where they continued as a band.

The last time that the Beatles recorded together was in August, 1969. The album released was *Abbey Road*, named after the street on which EMI studios is located. Ever since the release of that album, the world has referred to the studio as "Abbey Road". In fact, the sign over the doorway was changed from "EMI Studios" to "Abbey Road" in 1978. ∎

Behind these simple double doors the recordings were made. From Please, Please Me *to* Abbey Road: *a factory of hits.*

George Martin and the boys stop for refreshments in the lounge at EMI's Abbey Road Studios (left). On June 25, 1967 the Beatles performed All You Need is Love *representing Britain in the live video transmission of* Our World, *broadcast to twenty-four nations (below).*

Ad Lib Club

Leichester Place / Leichester Square

The Ad Lib Club was *the* watering hole for swinging London. In the mid-sixties the media helped create and then highlight a new society of London's younger and more liberal residents. Within this new circle were artists, fashion designers, models and, of course, pop stars needing a place to socialize and relax without the presence of annoying fans. Thus, the Ad Lib became their haven.

This social society of London's elite was high above London, in what is now a part of the Prince Charles Theater. Here, the Beatles, the Rolling Stones, Twiggy, and others mingled together to form the new caste–Pop-Royalty. ■

Apple Corps LTD.

Why Apple? Well why bloody not? The Beatles were the most popular act in the history of entertainment acts. They were art and now they wanted to be a business as well. This need was filled by the creation of The Apple.

A nice name Apple: fresh, fruity, clean, round, delicious, crisp, juicy, healthy, red, sometimes green and saucy. Apple–a perfect name to pick for a new company. And it looks better on a record label than a tongue.

The public's first taste of Apple came with an obscure acknowledgment on the back of the *Sgt. Pepper's* album crediting MC productions and The Apple. Little did anyone know

The crown Princes of Pop like to party in their spare time. To amuse themselves they would dress up in silly costumes and pretend to be things other than Beatles. Pictured below are three quarters of the fab-four, not at the Ad-Lib Club, but at the Royal Lancaster Hotel celebrating the completion of Magical Mystery Tour.

that this listing was the newly planted seed of what Richard Dillelo would call "The Longest Cocktail Party." Or that this company would evolve into a cavalcade of lawsuits and counter-lawsuits, many of which contributed to the dissolution of the Beatles as a group.

In May of 1968, Lennon and McCartney flew into New York City to announce the business ventures planned for their new company. Apple would be divided into five sub-companies: Apple Records, Apple Films, Apple Publishing, Apple Electronics and Apple Boutiques. The Beatles planned to use their wealth, power and influence to create what Paul McCartney called, "Western Communism." The company's proposed purpose was to help new and upcoming artists and musicians, hopefully preventing them from having to humiliate or compromise themselves to acquire backing and support for their projects.　□

Apple Boutique
94 Baker Street

In the tradition of Yves Saint Laurent, Christian Dior and Levi Strauss, the Beatles decided to enter the fashion industry. They commissioned four Dutch designers, known as *The Fool*, to create a line of contemporary clothing for the shop they planned to open.

A gala party opened the Apple Boutique on December 5, 1967, the first venture of what was to become a major experimental business creation. The building, located at the corner of Baker and Paddington streets, was decorated by a four-story psychedelic

Side-by-side comparisons of Apple's first retail venture. From psychedelic murals to stark white walls to please the neighborhood regulars. Either way, it never worked as planned (top). A handful of fans got away with free samples from the Beatles' boutique (bottom).

Apple Boutique
(continued)

mural also painted by *The Fool*. Colorful facial images, designs and shapes covered the outside brick walls. Needless to say, the conservative and narrow-minded neighbors sued to have the mural removed and replaced by a color more suitable to the area...like white! In spite of this new and more simplistic look, the boutique didn't last.

On July 30, 1968, the Beatles bailed out of the retail clothing business in true Beatles style. They gave all the clothes away for free–a £ 13,000 giveaway, which also created chaos in the streets of London.

□

The Apple boutique in its prime (above). Its current incarnation as a travel agency (right).

A music trade magazine ad promoting the newly refurbished Apple recording studios (left). When the Beatles began Apple, the model for the company's logo was the fresh, green Granny Smith apple (right).

Apple Studios

built for the needs of today with the foresight to encompass the needs of tomorrow

3 Savile Row London W.1. 01-734 3008

Apple
95 Wigmore Street

Two office suites within this building became the first home of the Beatles' new Apple Corps Ltd. in April of 1968. Right after the opening of their new headquarters, Ringo, his wife Maureen, Mal Evans, Peter Brown and Neil Aspinall were locked inside the building by an overzealous janitor. Shortly thereafter, Apple moved to its luxurious Savile Row location. □

George, looking very dapper, enjoys friendly conversation with some of the office staff inside the Savile Row building (below). The paint-chipped door and black iron-works are two views of Apple's Savile Row building as it looks today (opposite page). The front of the Wigmore Street office showing no signs of Beatlemania (far right).

Apple
3 Savile Row

On June 22, 1968, the Beatles purchased this five-story, Georgian townhouse for £500,000. Throughout that summer, Apple gradually moved into this luxurious location from both the Wigmore and Baker street addresses.

Savile Row is a short, narrow street (close to busy Regent Street) between Oxford and Piccadilly Circuses. It is the home of London's well-known and consistently conservative tailors, who were seriously disrupted when the Beatles and their surrounding hurricane moved in. Hurricane Apple hit hard! Not only was the neighborhood somewhat bothered by the fans, or "scruffs," converging near the southern end of Savile Row, but the confines of the office itself became a haven for all those who wanted to

Apple/Savile Row

(continued)

hang out and make their own "personal withdrawals."

The strongest department of Apple Corps was, naturally, the record division. With Apple's first release, *Hey Jude / Revolution*, the company exploded into a major new force in the record industry. The other slices of Apple did not share this success. It became apparent that it would take more than good vibes to run a successful business in a pretty building.

A recording studio was built in the basement of Savile Row by a so-called electronics wizard by the name of Magic Alex. Though he claimed to be building the ultimate recording studio, it never operated as planned. The Beatles had to finally request EMI to set up some portable recording equipment, until the studio could be redesigned. The middle section of the film, *Let It Be*, shows the band working out some tunes at this basement studio.

The party was over and so was the fun. By 1972 the building itself was physically collapsing. No one had considered the potential effects of moving and removing the beam supports when the basement studio was reconditioned. Apple was forced to move locations while 3 Savile Row waited for its facelift. This never happened.

Perhaps the most valuable souvenir from the Beatles' days on Savile Row is the film of them performing on its rooftop. It was their final performance in front of an audience: January 30, 1969. They passed the audition. Let it be. □

Apple

54 St. James Street
29 St. James Street

While badly needed repairs were to be made at Apple's Savile Row headquarters, the hurricane turned tropical storm converged on a new Apple "amusement park." This time at 54 St. James Street.

The Beatles disintegrated into solo artists: John, living in New York, never used the St. James office. Paul, having formed Wings, visited occasionally. So only Ringo and George utilized the facility frequently. Ringo's furniture design store, *Ringo or Robin*, opened on the ground floor with the remaining space used for Apple's offices, solo productions and various pet projects.

The building contractors took

Inside the gutted Savile Row building cement mixers begin to rebuild. The doorbell at today's Apple at 29 St. James Street.

Apple/St. James
(continued)

almost the rest of the decade to repair the aching Savile Row building, so Apple never returned. With the continuing decrease in the company's productivity, only a small business and accounting office was needed.

Apple soon moved across the street to its present home at 29 St. James Street. Today Apple is headed by Neil Aspinall, who still nurtures the remains of what was once the greatest "happy hour" in popular music.■

The Beatles' Fan Club
13 Manmouth Street

This London address was once the home of the Beatles Fan Club. Beatles fans arriving in London from around the world would congregate here to find out the latest Beatles news. The club started in 1962 in Liverpool and officially moved to London in 1968. It closed down in 1972. ∎

Beatles' Flats
Paul McCartney–Asher Flat–
* 57 Wimpole Street*
John Lennon–13 Emperor's Gate
George Harrison and Ringo Starr–
* Whaddon House, William Mews*
Ringo Starr–Montagu Square
Brian Epstein–13 Chapel Street

The Beatles were big and busy in 1963. They were constantly touring, recording or on the radio or television. Many of the BBC shows originated from London and all of their records were being made at EMI's St. John's Wood studio (see Abbey Road Studios, *London*). It was time for the Beatles to leave Liverpool and move into London. If international fame was to come, London would have to be the relay point.

Paul was the first to settle in London. Not in a flat of his own, but with his girlfriend's family. Earlier in 1963, Paul had met Jane Asher after a Beatles' concert (see Royal Albert Hall, *London*) and by the end of the year, he had moved into the Asher's Wimpole Street home. Paul lived here until 1966, when he purchased the Cavendish Street Estate (see McCartney's House, *London*).

John and his wife Cynthia moved into a flat in Kensington in the vicinity of the Royal Albert Hall in early 1964. They lived on Emperor's Gate with their son Julian, until they moved into their first home in the London suburb of Weybridge towards the end of 1964 (see Kenwood, *Daytripping*).

Being Beatle-bachelors, Ringo and George became roommates in this flat near Hyde Park. The building called Whaddon House on William Mews in Knightsbridge was the home for the two Beatles for a short time in early 1964. The street in front of the

Marble columns at 29 St. James where the present Apple accounting office is housed (opposite). Wimpole Street: Paul and Jane's old neighborhood (below).

Beatles' Flats
(continued)

flat was usually mobbed with fans who found out about this secret Beatles' bachelor pad. In April of 1964, the flat was burglarized and Ringo and George went their separate living ways.

Ringo moved into a new flat in Montagu Square. Adoring fans kept constant vigil outside this home, writing graffiti on the walls and nearby street signs. (This caused a problem for the Swiss Embassy which also was scrawled with Beatles' slogans.)

Ringo's flat was also used by John and Yoko, and on October 18, 1968, the classic couple were arrested for possession of hashish (see Marylebone Magistrate, *London*).

Brian Epstein obtained a flat on Chapel Street, near Buckingham Palace. Here he hosted many chic cocktail parties, including a press party for the Beatles' *Sgt. Pepper's Lonely Hearts Club Band* album. Brian died at his Chapel Street home on August 27, 1967 (see New London Synagogue, *London*). ■

The street sign in the posh Marylebone area where Ringo lived is covered with traditional Beatles graffiti (top). Brian Epstein at home in his fashionable Belgravia district home (below).

Buckingham Palace
The Mall

Buckingham Palace was originally built in the early 18th Century for John Sheffield, Duke of Buckingham and Normandy. It became the permanent home of the British Sovereign when Queen Victoria began residing at the palace. But it finally made a name for itself in 1965 when the Beatles were invited by Queen Elizabeth II to become Members of the British Empire, which allowed them discounts in many of London's theaters.

The event triggered quite a response throughout England. Many past recipients of the honor returned their medals in protest. Later, in 1969, John Lennon returned his MBE to protest Britain's interference in Biafra, America's involvement in Viet Nam and *Cold Turkey* slipping down the pop-charts.

This outstanding building made a substantial contribution to the Beatles' second feature film, *Help!* It was that "very famous palace," where the Beatles holed up in safety.

Most visitors to Buckingham Palace these days are attracted to the formal Changing Of The Guards which happens daily at 11:30 a.m. Though not exactly a Beatles' show, you can surely catch their mop-tops as they circle the front courtyard. Also, ask one of the guards if you can sign the Queen's guest book. Just one more thrill to round out your trip to another famous Beatles site. ∎

The Beatles display another set of trophies for their mums' and aunties' mantlepieces (above).

Carnaby Street
Soho

Many looked towards the Beatles for new ideas, trends and fashions during the mid-and late sixties. A fashion explosion occurred during those years, and the center of it was Carnaby Street. This hip lane runs parallel to Regent Street and sits in London's popular Soho district. At one time it was a most stylish strip, lined with fancy hair salons and boutiques. It became internationally known for catering to "swinging London."

However, as Carnaby Street became more famous, it became more commercialized. Today it is a somewhat tacky sidestreet full of tourist traps and clothing shops. Stacks of celebrity-etched mirrors are visible outside on the street. You'll probably find one with the faces of the Beatles printed over.

Stroll at your leisure, imagining what Carnaby Street must have been like during its golden years. The "Welcome to Carnaby Street" banner hangs across the main block reminding you just where you are. ∎

Decca Studios
165 Broadhurst Gardens

Well, Decca blew it! They had the Beatles in their studios, recording songs; ready, willing and able. All they had to do was say the word. In late 1961, the Beatles were the top club band in Northwestern England. Their new manager, Brian Epstein, was attempting to secure a recording contract for them (see HMV, *London* and NEMS, *Liverpool*). Decca Records was interested and, to their credit, agreed to an audition. So on December 31, 1961, the Beatles—John, Paul, George and Pete Best—along with their road manager, Neil Aspinall, rented a van and drove to London.

The audition was held on New Year's Day, 1962, in Decca's Hamstead Studio Number Three, with their artist and repertoire man, Mike

Decca Studios
(continued)

Smith. They recorded fifteen songs including a set of originals, rock-and-roll standards and a few pop classics. Paul McCartney sang: *Like Dreamers Do, Till There Was You, Sure to Fall, Love of the Loved, September in the Rain, Besame Mucho* and *Searchin'*. John Lennon sang: *Money, To Know Him Is to Love Him, Memphis* and *Hello Little Girl*. And George Harrison sang: *The Sheik of Araby, Take Good Care of my Baby, Three Cool Cats* and *Crying, Waiting, Hoping*.

When the audition was over, they returned to Liverpool and the Cavern Club and waited. Then they received the word. Decca Records, in one of the most infamous show business blunders since Twentieth Century-Fox turned down *Gone with the Wind*, declined to sign the Beatles. "Groups of guitars are on the way out," they replied. Eventually realizing their mistake, Decca signed the Rolling Stones. A logical second choice. The Stones became the "world's greatest rock-and-roll band" in 1970 by default. ∎

EMI House
20 Manchester Square

This bulky, geometric building is the world headquarters for EMI (Electrical and Musical Industries). It is the parent company for Parlaphone, on which the Beatles recorded. The glass facade was the background for the photograph on the cover of the Beatles' first British album, *Please, Please Me*.

In 1969, the Beatles, returning to their musical roots, intended to put together an album, calling it *Get Back*. Playing live in the studio as a basic quartet (with the addition of organist Billy Preston) they created a reunion of sorts without the high-tech gadgetry of previous studio efforts.

To help recreate this idea, the Beatles returned to the glass condo at EMI to photograph and imitate the cover of their first work. They stood together matching their original pose, this time with longer hair and individual attire. But they were too late. As a band, the Beatles were coming apart, and the album was eventually shelved.

This photograph for the *Get Back* project finally surfaced four years after the Beatles split up. Together with the original *Please, Please Me* photo, the two were used on the companion greatest hits anthologies that EMI released in 1974. ∎

A selection of Beatles hits not released by Decca Records.

FILM SITES
A Hard Day's Night

Throughout London one can find a number of locations used by the Beatles in their first two motion pictures. *A Hard Day's Night* was intended to be a low-budget, pop-exploitation film that the film studio would rush-release to coincide with the quick wave of Beatlemania. The Beatles act as themselves in a pseudo *cinema verité*-style romp throughout the streets and buildings of London.

Help!, on the other hand, was made as a big-budget, live-action "cartoon" shot in color in England and around the world. A few of the more curious and visible London locales from these

films are included here. (For other related points of cinematic Beatles interest, see: Buckingham Palace, Harrods, London Pavilion and Twickenham Film Studios–*London*. Also Stonehenge and West Malling Airfield–*Daytripping*). ☐

Paddington Train Station
Praed Street

As you walk into the Paddington train station, it is easy to visualize it as a black and white movie set, recalling the Beatles running through, being chased by throngs of screaming girls. The echoing ambience of the structure imitates that of a large Hollywood sound stage. The sleek, jet-black taxis still queue up in long rows, waiting perhaps, for the Beatles themselves to enter. The milk vending machines have long disappeared, but the photo booths are still around.

Each day during the filming of *A Hard Day's Night*, the Beatles and film crews began their day's journey from Paddington aboard a special train, filming the interior traveling sequences. And just as the opening scene was filmed at Paddington, so was their arrival after singing *I Should Have Known Better*. ☐

The Scala Theater
Charlotte Street

The Scala Theater, no longer in existence, was an abandoned building when it was discovered by the producers of *A Hard Day's Night*. Shortly thereafter it became the television studio seen in the film and the theater became the central locale for most of the picture. Screaming fans were added to union extras, all of whom were paid and fed. But who would care about food when the Beatles are live on stage in front of you? ☐

On the train at Paddington, the Beatles filming A Hard Day's Night *(opposite). A policeman prevents hysterical girls from forcing their way through the stage door of the Scala Theater where the Beatles are filming inside (below left). John, Paul, George, Ringo and Richard at St. Margaret's Field near Gatwick Airport (below right).*

Film Sites
(continued)

St. Margaret's Field

Can't Buy Me Love—a burst of beserk Beatles energy expressed in the sequence at St. Margaret's Field in the outskirts of London. Revolving around the large square map on a helicopter landing pad in *A Hard Day's Night*, John, Paul, George and Ringo dance, jump and fly off ladders from the sky, together and apart with magnificent, musical force.

Escaping from inside the theater, they briefly experience freedom as we can see from the aerial views. "I suppose you know this is private property." "Sorry if we hurt your field, mister." ∎

Ailsa Avenue
Twickenham

These famous four doors from *Help!* led into the Beatles' long, one-room apartment. It was architecturally amusing with a sunken bed, an organ that would pop up from beneath the floor and a wall of vending machines for fast-food service or quick (edible) defensive weapons (remember Ringo shooting whole oranges at his opponent during the assault on the Beatles' habitat?).

Obviously these front doors were only the exterior for the film studio interior. But who knows, maybe the current occupants knocked down a wall or two to recreate that Beatles atmosphere? □

Battersea Power Station
Near Battersea Park

If this were a *Pink Floyd Fan's Guide to England*, the Battersea Power Station just might be the most important listing in the book. Built in the early 1930s, this massive structure on the cover of Pink Floyd's *Animals* album is also the "well-known power station" we saw in the Beatles' *Help!*

Bringing electricity to much of greater London, Battersea is a must for those hooked on power. It took the "Relativity Cadenza" to slow things down in *Help!* and blow the royal fuse at Battersea. *Power to the People, Right On!* □

London Zoo
Regents Park

The London Zoo allows its visitors to observe the tigers through large glass windows. One of these yellow and black cats is named Raja. Once upon a time he escaped from his comfortable digs and crossed paths with Ringo in *Help!* But do not fear; Raja is harmless. A gift from the Berlin Zoo, he is said to sleep to Beethoven's "Ode to Joy" from the composer's famous *Ninth Symphony*. You can always try singing to all the tigers hoping to identify the real Raja: "Freude schoner Gotterfunken Tochter aus Elysium…" ∎

Battersea Power Station (top). Paddington Station (below).

Foyles Book Store
119 Charing Cross Road

As the largest bookstore in London and one of the best stocked stores in the world, Foyles has attracted a large, highly literate clientele. Many distinguished authors have been honored throughout the years by Foyles, so it would only be a short time until a Beatle was added to the list.

When John Lennon grew from a rock-and-roll musician into a well-respected author, Foyles sponsored a luncheon in honor of the release of his first book–the critically acclaimed classic, *In His Own Write*. When asked to make a speech, the reluctant and hungover Lennon simply muttered a fragmented, "Thank you." Everyone went home early. ∎

Fraser Gallery
69 Duke Street

On July 1, 1968, John Lennon presented his first public exhibition in a show called "You Are Here" at the Robert Fraser Gallery in Mayfair. Dedicated to Yoko Ono, the exhibit was a demonstration of avant-garde non-art; John's first attempt at being Yoko Ono.

The show consisted of a random

selection of charity collection boxes, a large white canvas with the printed words "You Are Here," and the release of 365 helium-filled balloons with cards attached that read: "You are here. Please write to John Lennon, c/o Robert Fraser Gallery, Duke Street, London W1." ∎

Harrods
Knightsbridge

One might call Harrods the Disneyland of department stores. It is London's, and maybe the world's, classiest merchandise emporium. As a tourist in London, one must gather together pence and pounds before heading towards Knightsbridge to spend a bit of time, and most likely money, "living in the material world."

Harrods sports crowded rooms and halls of traditional and off-beat fashions, toys, jewelry, electronics and even delightful delicacies at their gourmet shop. At Harrods you're bound to find something for yourself or someone you fancy.

Harrods will open after hours on occasion for those chosen few, royalty, wealthy businesspeople and once, for the Beatles themselves, allowing them to Christmas shop peacefully. Every department remained open as the four pursued their private buying spree, acquiring special surprises for those lucky enough to be on their Christmas lists.

In addition, visitors with keen eyes will certainly notice the green and gold Harrods' trucks making their way around London. One of these delivery vehicles was used in *Help!* by the High Priest Clang as he attempted to chase our heroes as they left their London apartment. Remember the secret agent music playing as the nails shot out onto the street from the special front exhaust pipe? What a truck! What a store! ∎

Heathrow Airport

It was Halloween Day in 1963. The Beatles returned to London from their successful Swedish tour to an amazing homecoming. Even Ed Sullivan and his wife were lost in the shuffle. They observed this demonstration of mass musical hysteria for the four popsters, and the chaotic experience naturally sparked the interest of the host of America's most popular television talent show. It certainly contributed to Sullivan's decision to feature the Beatles on his national broadcast on three consecutive Sundays in February of 1964. ∎

The Beatles return to London following their European tour, July 4, 1965 (top). Harrod's department store (bottom).

HMV Record Store
363 Oxford Street

HMV (His Master's Voice) is a large record shop located on London's busy Oxford Street. It is a department store of music, boasting four levels of records and tapes. And there is, after all, a Beatles' connection. First of all, the store usually carries the complete English catalogue of Beatles' albums as well as American, European and Japanese issues. Secondly, HMV is the main retail outlet for EMI which is the parent company for Parlaphone Records in England and Capitol Records in the United States. Thirdly, and most importantly, the store played a pivotal role in the beginning of the Beatles' recording career.

In May 1962, the Beatles were in Hamburg playing their premiere engagement at the new Star Club (see Hamburg, *Daytripping*). Back in

England, Brian Epstein was trying to secure the Beatles a recording contract. That January they recorded a demo tape for Decca Records (see Decca Records, *London*) which had been turned down. Brian carried the tape from record company to record company, all to no avail. After much pressure from his family to give up the band, Brian returned to London for one last-ditch effort to find a label for the Beatles. He was certain that it would be more professional and convenient if the tapes were pressed into discs. So Brian contacted a friend at HMV whom he thought might help accomplish this. Brian's friend introduced him to Syd Coleman, a music publisher, whose office was above HMV. Syd was excited about the tapes and played them for an A & R man at Parlaphone. He was George Martin, who subsequently signed and produced the Beatles (see Abbey Road Studios, *London*). And you thought that HMV was just another record shop. ∎

His Master's Voice logo (top). Window display promoting Paul's McCartney II *LP, May, 1980 (bottom).*

Indica Gallery
Mason's Yard

"The Destruction of Art" was the title of the symposium that attracted Yoko Ono to England in 1966. Yoko's bag was conceptual art, which meant she went around doing silly things. For conceptual artists the idea behind a piece, and the subsequent process of creation, is equal to, or more important than, the actual object once finished.

Yoko caused quite a stir by wrapping sheets around the stone lions in Trafalgar Square and later photographing a series of naked bottoms.

In November of 1966, she presented a show titled "Unfinished Paintings and Objects by Yoko Ono" at John Dunbar's Indica Gallery. Dunbar, who was once married to singer Marianne Faithfull, invited John Lennon to the show's opening as a potential sponsor of future exhibits, and to meet Yoko.

On the night of the opening, Yoko walked up to John Lennon and shyly handed him a card that simply read: BREATHE. In response, John puffed and panted, much to Yoko's delight. Artistically, a spark was lit. ■

A graphic display of John's "obscene" art.

Lisson Gallery
68 Bell Street

Yoko Ono introduced her own hemisphere to London in 1967 with her art show at the Lisson Gallery called "The Half Wind Show." Every work displayed was "a half" of something. There was half of a table and half a chair—all household items that were cut in half.

John Lennon's interest in unusual expression resulted in his financing the show. Though Yoko wanted John's name to appear in the exhibition's catalogue next to hers, John refused. Instead, he worked up the catalogue's name, *Yoko Plus Me*. ■

London Arts Gallery
22 New Bond Street

In January 1970, John Lennon's collection of erotic lithographs was exhibited at the London Arts Gallery. This was the first showing of the fourteen drawings depicting images of John and Yoko's wedding, bed-in and personal activities. Three hundred sets of the fourteen lithographs were made and packaged in large, white, leather carrying cases, each labeled "Bag One" with John's autograph. Each of the total three thousand prints were individually signed by John as well.

During the second day of the show, the London Gallery was raided by the police and eight of the lithographs were confiscated as "obscene." When the case went to court, drawings by Picasso were produced for comparison, and John Lennon's famous lithographs were then considered "fine art." The case was closed and the prints returned. ∎

John and Yoko's honeymoon on display (top). Unfinished photograph number one: a sample of conceptual art (left).

London Palladium
8 Argyll Street

Another milestone: Sunday, October 13, 1963, the Beatles appeared on the television variety show *Sunday Night at the London Palladium*, which was broadcast live from this Argyll Street venue. From this date, the press jumped on the Beatles bandwagon, reporting a riot of thousands of fans obstructing the streets around the theater. The Beatles became front page favorites, brightening the often mundane headlines in newspapers throughout England. ■

Paul and Zsa Zsa Gabor along with 98 other performers appeared at the London Palladium in the benefit show, Night of 100 Stars, July 23, 1964 .

London Pavilion

3 Piccadilly Circus

The last visible demonstration of full-scale Beatlemania occurred on July 17, 1968 outside the London Pavilion at the premiere of the animated feature, *Yellow Submarine*. The theater had previously been the center of this mania during the premiere of *A Hard Day's Night* on July 6, 1964, *Help!* on July 29, 1965

London Pavilion
(continued)

and Richard Lester's satirical *How I Won the War* (featuring John Lennon as the peculiar Army Private Gripweed) on October 18, 1967. *Let It Be* opened on May 20, 1970, without the hoopla of their previous efforts.

The Pavilion, located on busy Piccadilly Circus, is London's most famous film theater. At night the well-lit, white building dominates the intersection that is often compared to New York's neon-sign-filled Times Square. The London Pavilion was built many years ago by a lot of men with tools, and has been a theater ever since. ∎

Rock films still debut at the London Pavilion (above). The Beatles arrive for the premiere of A Hard Day's Night *(right).*

Lyceum

Wellington Near Strand

In the winter of 1969, Delaney and Bonnie along with Eric Clapton made their first tour of Great Britain. Joining them on stage for some of the shows was George Harrison, and when they played a benefit for UNICEF at the Lyceum on December 15, 1969, Delaney and Bonnie, Eric Clapton and George Harrison backed up John and Yoko and transformed into the Plastic Ono Band for the night.

"Peace for Christmas" was the name of the show, and it was John's first concert performance in Britain since the Beatles played Wembley Empire Pool in 1966 (see Wembley, *London*). It was also the first time that any two Beatles performed together live since their last-ever concert in San Francisco on August 29, 1966.

The results of this Lyceum show can be heard on side three of John and Yoko's *Sometime in New York City* album.   ■

Madame Tussaud's Wax Museum
Marylebone Road at Baker Street

On the back cover of the album *Sgt. Pepper's Lonely Hearts Club Band* reads the credit: "Wax figures by Madame Tussaud's." They stand on the cover looking younger than ever amongst their friends and heroes. These four wax figures of an earlier incarnation of the Liverpool lads look like schoolboys, propped up next to their new, real-life, colorful forms.

In their collarless suits, the moptops became one of the most popular attractions at the famous wax palace. As the real Beatles changed, so did the dress and facial appearances of their wax look-alikes. Mustaches were added, John received a pair of wire-rimmed glasses and they were clothed in psychedelic garb to parallel their newly found image.

In 1968, entirely new wax figures were cast and exhibited. The new look was taken from their *White Album* phase. Once again their faces were clean shaven and their attire, though simple, was colorful. ■

Marylebone Magistrate / Registrar's Office
181 Marylebone Road

The photograph on the back cover of John and Yoko's *Life with the Lions* album documents the beginning of John's difficulties with the United States Immigration Department. It was taken in front of the Marylebone Magistrate Court. On October 18, 1968, John and Yoko were arrested for possession of hashish in the Montagu Square flat of Ringo Starr (see Beatles' Flats, *London*). The next day, appearing at Marylebone Magistrate, John pleaded guilty and the charges against Yoko were dropped. Although John maintained that the drugs were planted, he was advised to plead guilty and pay a fine to avoid having charges brought against Yoko, who would have been deported if convicted. She was pregnant at the time.

He later regretted this decision, as it was the crux of the case by the United States Immigration Department which wanted to deport John back to England. After years of legal battles,

Marylebone
(continued)

the conviction of the officer who busted John and Yoko for planting drugs on others and the end of the Nixon era, John Lennon finally obtained his green card, allowing him to reside in the United States.

In the same building on Marylebone Road at the Registrar's Office, Paul McCartney married Linda Eastman on March 12, 1969 and Ringo Starr and Barbara Bach tied the knot on April 26, 1981. ∎

The continuing story of Beatlemania, now in its third decade, on the occasion of Ringo's marriage to Barbara Bach. In attendance at the event were Paul and Linda and George and Olivia (above). John and Yoko leave court (bottom right).

McCartney's House
7 Cavendish

After visiting Abbey Road Studios you'll probably want to visit Paul's home in St. John's Wood. It is only a short, five-minute walk from the Abbey Road crosswalk and studios (see Abbey Road, *London*).

The St. John's Wood district of London is an upper middle-class residential neighborhood. Paul's large, three-story home is surrounded by an eight-foot wall with green metal gates. It was painted in faded pinks, reds, yellows and blues, looking very unkept, but was renovated in 1980.

Paul bought the house in 1966 for £ 40,000 to become London's only Beatle-in-residence, as the others purchased homes just outside the city. Because Cavendish is within walking distance of Abbey Road Studios, Paul's home became a frequent meeting place for the Beatles before many of their recording sessions. John and Paul used an upstairs workroom to put finishing touches on many tunes. ■

MPL Communications

1 Soho Square

Here at Soho Square is the main headquarters for Paul's business affairs and publishing empire, McCartney Productions, Ltd., or simply MPL. Paul has kindly placed MPL across from a beautiful and quiet little park that centers the square, making it a wonderful location to sit and relax and possibly catch a glimpse of the company's owner and namesake.

From this five-story Georgian townhouse, Paul's company controls the publishing rights to not only McCartney's own compositions, but also those of Buddy Holly, Scott Joplin, Ira Gershwin, and the musical scores to such Broadway hits as *A Chorus Line*, *Grease* and *Annie*. This impressive collection makes MPL the largest independent music publishing company in the world today.

In the late 1970s, Paul had a recording studio built in the basement of

this Soho Square office building. The studio is a replica of Paul's favorite recording studio, Abbey Road's Studio Number Two.

Friday is garbage night at Soho Square. Large plastic, bulky bags of throwaways are piled next to the entrances and side doors of the office buildings that surround the square, waiting to be collected early the next morning by garbage trucks, or late that night by scavenging Beatles fanatics and garbologists. ∎

The house that Michelle, Eleanor, Rita, Martha, Mother Mary, Peggy Sue, Annie and famous groupies built.

New London Synagogue
33 Abbey Road

On October 17, 1967, five weeks after the death of Brian Epstein, a memorial service was held for him at the New London Synagogue, just up the street from Abbey Road Studios. The funeral in Liverpool had been a private, family affair, but the memorial service was shared by friends and business relations. All four of the Beatles were in attendance. ■

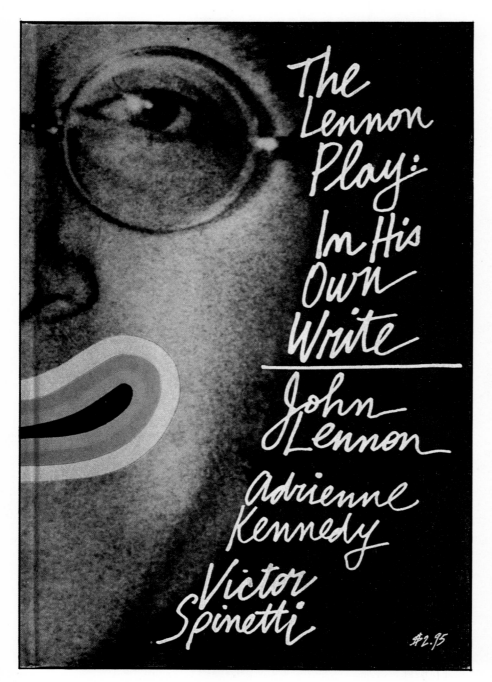

The Lennon Play:
In His Own Write

John Lennon
Adrienne Kennedy
Victor Spinetti

$2.95

Old Vic Theater
Waterloo Road

Our story takes place on June 18, 1968, in a classic old theater near Waterloo Station on the south bank of the Thames. The theater, called the Old Vic, is the home of the National Theater Company. It is opening night, the house is full. The audience is quiet. Behind the stage stands the director, Victor Spinetti, star of screen gems such as *A Hard Day's Night, Help!* and the devastating *Magical Mystery Tour.* In the audience is the author of the book on which the play is based, John Lennon. He sits next to Japanese artist, Yoko Ono–a pairing which causes a flurry of rumors and speculation since John's wife, Cynthia, is nowhere in sight. This is John and Yoko's first public outing together.

The curtain rises and for the next couple of hours, *In His Own Write* is performed to an attentive crowd. Spinetti, Lennon and the play's co-author, Adrienne Kennedy, nervously watch their creation come to life. ■

Prince of Wales Theater
31 Coventry Street

"Thank you. For our last number I'd like to ask your help. Would the people in the cheaper seats clap your hands. And the rest of you, if you'll just rattle your jewelry. Thank you. We'd like to sing a song called Twist and Shout." (John Lennon from the Royal Command Performance, November 4, 1963.)

Based on the overwhelming success of their appearance on the nationally televised program *Sunday Night at the London Palladium,* the

Beatles were asked to appear at the Prince of Wales Theater, on the occasion of the annual Royal Command Performance. The bill included such acts as Marlene Dietrich and Tommy Steele, but the Beatles were the obvious stars of the show.

In the Royal Box sat Her Majesty, the Queen Mother, Princess Margaret and Lord Snowdon, who were amused by the Beatles' irreverent comments.

The Beatles performed four songs for the show, *She Loves You, Till There Was You, From Me to You* and *Twist and Shout*. ■

The Beatles still make front page headlines (top left). Prince of Wales Theater (above).

Queen Charlotte's Hospital
339 Goldhawk

The first release of Apple Record's experimental offshoot, Zapple Records, was John and Yoko's *Unfinished Music No. 2: Life with the Lions*. Side two of the album was actually recorded here in their hospital room prior to Yoko's miscarriage in November of 1968.

John and Yoko shared a hospital room at Queen Charlotte's, where they recorded a series of avant-garde tracks, some reminiscent of Gregorian chants. As the hospital became short of beds, John relinquished his and slept on the floor in a sleeping bag, as you can see on the cover of the *Lions* album.

Ringo and his wife, Maureen, shared some brighter moments at Queen Charlotte's, where all three of their children were born. Two sons, Zak on September 13, 1965 and Jason on August 19, 1967 and a daughter, Lee, on November 17, 1970. ■

Radha Krishna Temple
Soho Street at Soho Square

HAVE LUNCH WITH APPLE RECORDING ARTISTS!

Once a week the public is invited to lunch and a general "be-in" and meditation of sorts at the headquarters of the Krishna Society in London. George Harrison, the well known Krishna crusader, invited the saffron-robed devotees to the basement recording studio at Apple's Savile Row offices, to cut a creative and enjoyable album of Hare Krishna chants.

The album was released on Apple Records in May of 1971. Hare rama, hare rama; rama, rama, hare, hare. ■

Royal Albert Hall
Kensington Gore

Now they know how many holes it takes to fill the Albert Hall.

These lyrics from *A Day in the Life* represent the primary reason that

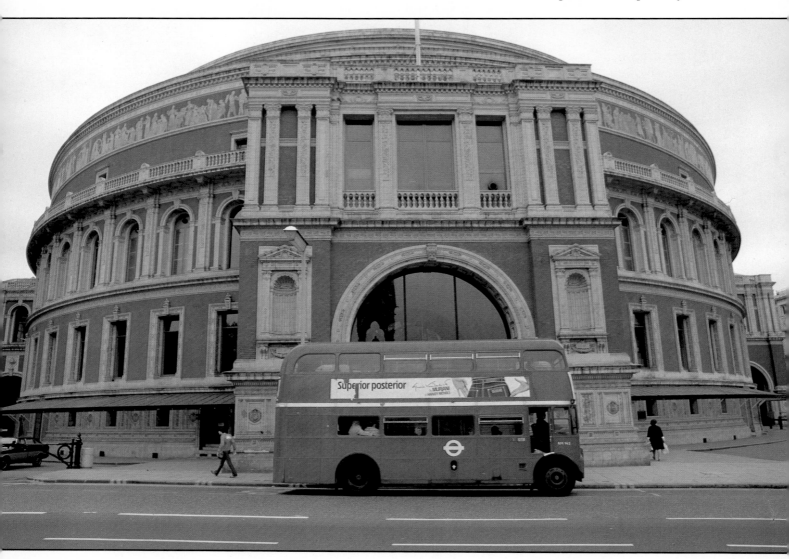

any self-respecting Beatles fan would bother to visit the Royal Albert Hall.

Although this beautiful, circular arena holds great historical, cultural and social importance, Beatles fans should make note of the major events that took place here. On May 9, 1963, Paul met Jane Asher after the Beatles performed at the Hall and the two were considered "an item" for a number of years.

In one of their more imaginative events, John and Yoko sat in a huge

Royal Albert Hall
(continued)

black bag on the stage of this London landmark built in 1871. The occasion was the Alchemical Wedding: A Christmas party in 1968 put on by *The Underground*, a group of artists. ∎

Trident Studios
17 St. Annes Court

Some believe that all of the Beatles' records were recorded at EMI's Abbey Road Studios. But in October of 1968, sessions for what was to become the Beatles' *White Album* were moved to Trident Studios in Soho. The tracks recorded on Trident's newly installed eight-track board were *Honey Pie*, *Dear Prudence*, *Savoy Truffle* and *Martha My Dear*. ∎

Twickenham Film Studios
The Barons, Twickenham

Picture if you will, a huge, cold, cavernous room; a sound-stage for making moving pictures. A large 180° backdrop lit with multi-colored lights, creating depth and interest to

Carriage entrance, Royal Albert Hall (left). Trident Studios, Soho (top). Twickenham Film Studios (bottom).

an otherwise uninteresting visual. Through the grainy film we can see the four Beatles, more separate than together, huddled around their various instruments, amplifiers, microphones and scaffolding. Dressed warmly, they are working on sections of songs, some sounding very rough and sloppy. John and Yoko waltz across the floor to the tune of George's *I Me Mine*, in ¾ time.

This is the filming of what would eventually become known as *Let It Be*. The location is the Twickenham Film Studios. Located in the outskirts of London, this film production facility was also used by the Beatles for some of the interior shots for *Help!* and *A Hard Day's Night*, as well as the promotional films for *Hey Jude* and *Revolution*. ∎

An apple a day keeps the doctor away (sometimes).

University College Hospital
Gower Street

Inside of our mouths many of us have a pair of oval masses composed mainly of lymphoid tissue and covered with mucuous membrane. These are called tonsils. Ringo doesn't have his and neither does George. On December 2, 1964, Ringo's tonsils were removed at the University College Hospital. During his stay, he proposed marriage to Maureen Cox. They were married on February 11, 1965. George Harrison acquired an inflammation of the tonsils and had his removed here on February 7, 1969. The tonsils are located one on each side of the back of the mouth leading to the pharynx, and are supposed to act as sources for the supply of phagocytes to the mouth and pharynx. ∎

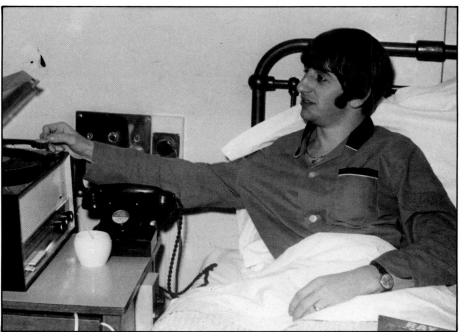

Wall's Ice Cream

While in England there are two gastronomical temptations that cannot be avoided. The first is Wimpy's–a famous European fast-food hamburger chain. It is a well-known fact that there are more Wimpy's than there are holes in the Albert Hall, making it very easy to stumble across one.

The second delight is Wall's Ice Cream. Pre-packed bars of icy chocolate pleasure, wrapped in colorful paper that satisfies one's need for sweets (for sure you'll stumble across Wall's or most likely trip over one of the bright A-framed adverts that seem to occupy every street corner in London).

On July 18, 1969, Wall's Ice Cream briefly merged with the Beatles' Apple Corps Ltd. to issue a special promotional extended-play record featuring four songs by new Apple recording artists. The EP included *Something's Wrong* by James Taylor, *Little Yellow Pills* by Jackie Lomax, *Happiness Runs (Pebble and the Man)* by Mary Hopkins and *Storm in a Teacup* by the Iveys, who later were known as Badfinger. The record, now a very rare one indeed, was given away at London's West End ice cream shops. ∎

Wembley Empire Pool
Empire Way

It was here at Wembley Empire Pool that the Beatles gave their final British concert. Although they didn't know it at the time, May 1, 1966 would mark their farewell performance to England. The concert was the *New Music Express* pollwinners. The Beatles topped the bill with such acts as the Rolling Stones, Cliff Richard, the Who, the Yardbirds, the Spencer Davis Group, the Small Faces, Herman's Hermits and Roy Orbison. ∎

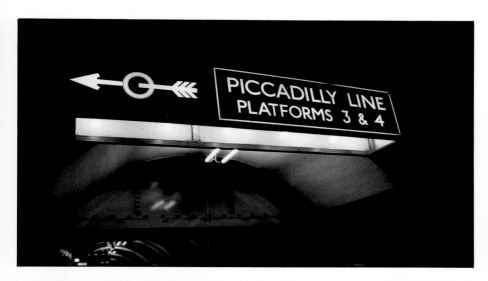

Mathew Street, Liverpool

Liverpool

A Seaport City   International trade   ships and sailors
ferry across the Mersey   docks   industrial   blue
suburban skies   Angelican Cathedral   coffee bars and
clubs   the cave   chip butties and pints   more greasy
fish and chips   tree lined streets   spacious green parks
middle class   working class   rebuilt war-torn town
the Empire Theater   shopping districts   Beatle birthplaces.

Liverpool

BIRTHPLACES

Richard Starkey
9 Madryn Street
John Winston Lennon
Liverpool Maternity Hospital
Oxford Street
James Paul McCartney
Walton General Hospital
107 Rice Lane
George Harrison
12 Arnold Grove

On the ancient Emerald Tablets found inside the great Pyramids over four thousands years ago, it is written that "four scarabs will one day walk the Earth, spreading joy and wisdom throughout the world. From that day on, nothing else will ever be the same." These scarabs, or Beatles as they were to be called, did not come from Egypt, where these great stone structures stand, but from a seaport in the Northwest corner of England: Liverpool.

Ringo's birthplace (left). John's birthplace (right).

The Beatles came one by one. First, on July 7, 1940 in a small, four-room brick row house on Madryn Street, Richard Starkey was born. The neighborhood, far from majestic, is a lower-class area of hard-working people. It is called the Dingle.

The Liverpool Maternity Hospital is across town situated closer to the city center. John Winston arrived here on October 9, 1940. It took another two years before the formula could be added to. James Paul McCartney made us wait until June 18, 1942 before he appeared at the Walton General Hospital.

The hand was now almost fully dealt and the next year, George Harrison, being the youngest, finally arrived on February 25, 1943. He was born in a small house on Arnold Grove, in a neighborhood similar to that of Ringo's. ■

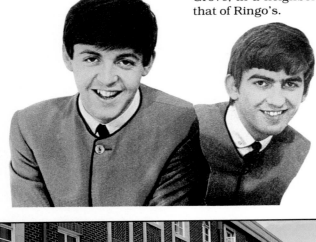

Paul's birthplace (left). George's birthplace (right).

CHILDHOOD HOMES

John Lennon
9 Newcastle
251 Menlove
3 Gambier Terrace

John lived briefly at 9 Newcastle near Penny Lane with his mother Julia. His father, Freddy, had gone away to sea, abandoning both John and Julia. Since Julia's sister Mimi, and her husband, George Smith, had no children of their own, they raised John in their home at 251 Menlove.

Menlove is a wide and busy boulevard, scattered with trees and parks. Simple, freestanding homes line both sides of the suburban street. John's Menlove house is the nicest of all the Beatles' childhood homes. Bay windows open onto a small, front garden surrounded by hedges and fencing intended to insulate the residents from busy street traffic. Just a short distance away, at a nearby intersection on Menlove, Julia Lennon, crossing the street towards her bus stop, was struck and killed by a car driven by an off-duty policeman. It happened on July 15, 1958.

In early 1960, John Lennon and Stuart Sutcliffe moved into a flat at 3

Gambier Terrace. The long Victorian building overlooks the awesome Anglican Cathedral and is very close to the Liverpool Art Institute which John attended. This large, untidy flat became a gathering place for the institute's students and John's musical friends. After a short time, John moved back with his Aunt Mimi until the Beatles embarked on their first trip to Hamburg, Germany that August. □

Aunt Mimi's Menlove home (far left). John and Stu's Gambier Terrace flat (left). An early publicity shot by Dezo Hoffman of the Beatles in Paul's backyard at Forthlin Street (right).

Childhood Homes
(continued)

Paul ironing things out at his home on Forthlin (above and right).

Paul McCartney
12 Ardwick Road
20 Forthlin

During most of Paul's schooling, the McCartneys lived in a small city-owned house at 12 Ardwick Road. In 1955, Jim and Mary McCartney, with their sons Paul and Michael, moved into a nicer home at 20 Forthlin. Inside the house was a piano, played by Paul's father, who performed in jazz bands. This musical interest of the elder McCartney definitely influenced Paul to pursue his own musical development.

In 1956, Mary McCartney died of cancer. Jim McCartney raised his two sons with the help of friends and relatives. From then on, Paul's interest in music grew and he was encouraged by his father to take up the guitar.

The house at 20 Forthlin became mobbed with fans as the Beatles became Liverpool music stars. Paul lived here until the Beatles moved to London in 1963. ❑

George Harrison
12 Arnold Grove
25 Upton Green
174 Mackets Lane

Of all the Beatles, George's early years were most tranquil. His family

did not suffer the pains of death or separation. By remaining on government housing lists, the family was able to improve their living environment with each of many moves.

After George was born on Arnold Grove, the Harrison family moved to 25 Upton Green in Liverpool's Speke district. This house, located at one end of a large circular street with a grass field in its middle, was the Harrison's home until about 1959. George played the guitar for the first time within the walls of his Upton Green home. On one of his many bus rides to school, George met Paul McCartney who was one grade ahead of him at the same school.

The family's next move was to a larger house, closer to the city's center, at 174 Mackets Lane. George's mother, Louise, encouraged George and his musician friends to practice at their Mackets Lane home. Both the Quarrymen and the Beatles rehearsed here. ☐

Upton Green, where George first played the guitar (top). The Quarrymen and the Beatles would practice at Mackets Lane (bottom).

Childhood Homes
(continued)

Ringo Starr
9 Madryn Street
10 Admiral Grove
Myrtle Children's Hospital
  Myrtle Street at Mulbert

An unfortunate tale of physical suffering influences the list of Ringo's childhood homes. He lived in a poor neighborhood called the Dingle. Rows and rows of small brick buildings make up this area where Ringo spent his childhood. He first lived at his birthplace on Madryn Street and then his family moved to another, smaller house at 10 Admiral Grove, less than two blocks away.

When Ringo was six, he spent a full year as a resident of the Myrtle Street Children's Hospital after developing peritonitis from a ruptured appendix. He returned home to his mother Elsie, a divorcee who was now married to Harry Graves, a house painter for the city of Liverpool. In 1953, Ringo returned to the hospital, this time for a two-year stay for treatment of pleurisy. ■

Admiral Grove in the Dingle: typical government row houses (top left). The Myrtle Street Hospital (left). Dovedale Primary School (right).

LIVERPOOL SCHOOLS

Dovedale Primary
Dovedale Road

Although both John and George attended Dovedale Primary at the same time, they didn't know each other since George was two grades below John. Their paths probably did cross however, as each was escorted by a doting relative on the bus ride to Dovedale, which is very near to Penny Lane.

While attending Dovedale, John began writing and drawing, developing his unique and irresistible style. Some of these crayon creations from 1952 were later preserved on the cover of his 1974 *Walls and Bridges* album. □

Liverpool Schools
(continued)

St. Silas Primary
8 High Park Street

Dingle Vale Secondary Modern
Dingle Vale Street

Ringo's education was constantly interrupted by sickness. He first attended St. Silas Primary located in his own neighborhood. At the end of his first year he left school and entered the hospital, returning to his studies a year later.

In 1951, Ringo began school at Dingle Vale Secondary Modern. He was a student here for a mere two years until another illness returned him to the hospital. After the age of fifteen, school interests were over as Ringo was far behind in every scholarly way.

A few years later when Ringo attempted to obtain his school records, he found that as far as Dingle Vale was concerned, he had never existed. Of course, once Ringo became a famous Beatle, the school placed a desk on display claiming it was once Ringo's. And, for a small fee, a visitor could have a photo taken sitting at the desk. □

Stockton Wood Road Primary
Speke

Joseph Williams Primary
Gateacre

Of all the Beatles, Paul was the most interested in his early education. At least that was what his grades showed. They were the best of the band, as he received high marks in most of his subjects.

He began at Stockton Wood Primary in 1948. It is a Protestant school located in Liverpool's Speke district. When the school became overcrowded, he was transferred to Joseph Williams Primary in Gateacre near Woolton and finally placed at the Liverpool Institute where he would befriend George Harrison. □

Quarry Bank Grammar
Harthill Road

Quarry Bank is one of the most prestigious of Liverpool's high schools. Its brick walls and steep roof adorned with vines of ivy add to its respected educational reputation.

John entered Quarry Bank in 1952, majoring in "Trouble." He became the class clown with his new friend and partner in crime, Pete Shotten (who would later manage the Beatles' Apple Boutique, see *London*). John continued to work on his writing, constantly putting pen to paper, resulting in outrageous stories from his own inventive mind.

In 1954, while still a student at Quarry Bank, rock-and-roll was introduced to John by way of Bill Haley's *Rock Around The Clock* and the American explosion of Elvis Presley. All of this inspired John to form his own skiffle group, calling it the Quarrymen. □

Quarry Bank Grammar School (below).

Liverpool Schools
(continued)

Liverpool Institute
Liverpool Art Institute
Hope Street/Mount Street

The Liverpool Institute is the oldest and most respected of all the Liverpool schools. Its tall, stone pillars give it a more stately appearance than Quarry Bank, which can only boast a few bricks and lots of funky ivy. Built in the 1830s as a school of mechanics, the Institute and the Art College were one and the same. They later separated and created two independent institutions.

John enrolled at the Art Institute in 1957 after his mediocre performance at Quarry Bank. He met Cynthia Powell here the next year in a lettering class and the two were married on August 23, 1962.

In 1959, John befriended another talented art student–Stuart Sutcliffe. Stuart's artistic flair and dress influenced John dramatically. This friendship renewed John's interest in his studies.

At the same time, Paul and George were attending the Liverpool Institute next door to the art school. Together with John, the three were the remaining members of the Quarrymen. They frequently skipped classes to occupy the nearby pubs and coffeehouses.

Paul and George's High School: The Liverpool Institute (left).

By mid-1960, John, Paul and George had completed their formal education and were about to make their first trip to Hamburg. George flunked out the previous year, having failed all of his General Certificate of Education examinations except for Art (he worked at Blackler's Department Store as an electrician for awhile). Paul barely completed his studies and John's interest in art school was next to nil. Though formally registered at the school, John rarely attended class. The challenge of a musical trip to Hamburg came at a most opportune time. ■

Paul poses with his geography teacher, Bertram Parker, after a special concert by Paul for the Liverpool Institute (right).

An example of the art (above) of Stuart Sutcliffe, a student with John at the Liverpool Art Institute (left).

LIVERPOOL CLUBS

In Liverpool, a number of clubs and ballrooms came and went as did the bands themselves. In the late fifties and early sixties the music scene in Liverpool was steaming with activity. Any structure capable of holding more than a couple of dozen people was converted into a musical showcase; storefronts, gymnasiums, recreation halls, basements, warehouses and even church social halls became newborn clubs. Some have played major roles in the history of the music, such as the Cavern Club. Others, like the Grafton, Aintree and the Realto also added to the development of the club scene and the evolution of bands like the Beatles. ☐

Casbah Club
8 Haymans Green, West Derby

In 1938, a film called *Algiers* with Heddy Lamarr and Charles Boyer gave birth to the infamous line, "Come with me to the Casbah" (a phrase never actually said in the film). Pete Best's mother remembered the words anyway and decided to name her basement club the Casbah. The darkness within the club reminded her of old Algiers.

In 1959, Pete Best wanted to clear out the basement of the family's large West Derby home and convert it into a social hall for entertaining friends. Mona Best, expanding on her son Pete's idea, and attempting to help his shy social life, turned the basement into a private coffee club with music and refreshments for teenagers.

The Casbah's opening act in August of 1959 was the Quarrymen, consisting of John Lennon, Paul McCartney, George Harrison and Ken Brown. Three hundred people showed up and both the group and the club were hits.

Constant exposure to the music and life of the club inspired Pete Best to become a musician himself. He began fooling around with an old drum kit left inside the Casbah. When Ken Brown left the Quarrymen, the two started their own band called the Blackjacks. The Quarrymen, now John, Paul, George and Stuart Sutcliffe, had become the Silver Beatles and moved on to somewhat larger and more lucrative engagements in the Liverpool area.

The Blackjacks became the Casbah's house band, but soon disbanded leaving Pete back at the club, until he was invited by Paul to join the Beatles prior to the band's journey to Hamburg.   □

In the early sixties the Beatles performed at dozens of clubs throughout Liverpool, including the Aintree Institute on Longmoor Lane (top and left) and the Grafton Ballroom on West Derby Road (bottom right).

Liverpool Clubs
(continued)

Jacaranda Club
23 Slater Street

Blue Angel Club
8 Seel Street

Allan Williams, alias *The Man Who Gave The Beatles Away* (the title of his book), operated two clubs–The Jacaranda and the Blue Angel. As a man who had been involved in many

musically related activities, Williams laid the groundwork for the Beatles' Hamburg visits (see Hamburg, *Day-tripping*).

Williams first opened the Jacaranda, a coffee bar where Liverpool's Bohemian crowd would hang out. Amongst these in 1959 were the Beatles, musicians and art students themselves, who spent a lot of time at the Jac, as it was referred to. One of the specialties at the Jac was "bacon butties," an English culinary delight made up of bacon and butter stuck between two bland pieces of white bread. One of these with coffee or a soft drink would sustain one's appetite for awhile.

Downstairs in the basement was a dance floor where a West Indies steel drum band played. During the days the Quarrymen/Moondogs/Silver Beatles or whatever their name was at the time, used this space for rehearsals. They were also commissioned by Allan Williams to paint murals throughout the club when the time came for remodeling. The murals are long gone.

Since the Jac was successful and attractive as a hangout, a second club was opened by Allan Williams. He attempted to present a club with true decor contrasting the bareness of the

The Jac as it looks today (left) and its original sign, once above the doorway, now made into a coffee table (top).

The famous photograph of the Beatles auditioning for Larry Parnes in Allan Williams' Blue Angel Club in April of 1960 (left).

Blue Angel
(continued)

The Blue Angel Club today (above). Views of the Litherland Town Hall (opposite page).

Jac. This new club was called The Blue Angel.

Shortly after the Blue Angel opened, Williams allowed promoter Larry Parnes to use the club to audition bands to back up singer Billy Fury on a concert tour. The Silver Beatles, consisting of John, Paul, George, Stuart Sutcliffe and drummer Johnny Hutchinson who sat in, auditioned for Parnes. He liked the band, but wanted them to perform without Stuart on bass. The boys refused. Later Parnes was impressed enough to allow them to back another singer, Johnny Gentle, on a tour of Scotland. This became their first professional concert tour. □

Litherland Town Hall
Hatton Hill Road

As far as the Beatles were concerned, their first trip to Hamburg was a disaster (see Kaiserkeller-Hamburg, *Daytripping*). George was deported by the German government for being under age and the disillusioned members of the band individually drifted home to Liverpool. They were broke and not really sure if they were still a band. For the first few weeks after they returned, they kept separate while they allowed their digestive tracks to recover from some of the würst food they had ever ingested.

Bob Wooler, who was then the disc-jockey at the Cavern Club, organized a welcome home show for the Beatles on December 27, 1960 at the Litherland Town Hall. The hall was used for town meetings, social gatherings and bi-weekly teen dances. It was the

Litherland
(continued)

largest place that the Beatles had played up to that time.

The standard of pop music in England at that time was Cliff Richard and the Shadows. They wore matching slick outfits neatly arranged, and motioned to the music with catchy unison dance steps. The Beatles were everything that the Shadows weren't. The shock of the new, carrying on like no other band around. The Litherland gig that night exploded as the Beatles presented to Liverpool an almost totally new form of themselves that had developed strongly throughout their months spent in Hamburg. They were still rough-looking Teddy Boys in boots and black leather, but their sound had changed, making them one of Liverpool's tightest rock-and-roll bands.

All of the excitement and energy brought about a riot on that night. To the local fans and to the Beatles themselves, everything had finally come together. There now was no looking back as the Beatles gathered momentum and began to generate their own important sound. □

Litherland Urban District Council
NOTICE
ADMISSION or RE-ADMISSION TO THE BALL-ROOM IS NOT ALLOWED AFTER 9 pm. THE ENTRANCE DOOR WILL BE CLOSED AT THAT TIME AND OPENED ONLY FOR THE PURPOSE OF PERMITTING PEOPLE TO LEAVE THE BUILDING.

The Cavern Club
10 Mathew Street

The Cavern Club opened in 1957 as a jazz club. It was located underneath a warehouse in what used to be a wine cellar, 18 steps below street level, making it dark and stuffy with terrible ventilation. The three brick archways and walls were a perfect match to the cobblestones that made up Mathew Street.

The club was taken over in 1959 by Ray McFall who slowly allowed skiffle groups to appear on the bills as open-

Cavern Club

(continued)

ing acts. The Blue Genes were the first non-jazz group to play the Cavern, and the beat groups began playing lunchtime sessions. Later they progressed to the evenings and eventually took over the entire venue.

The Beatles were one of these beat groups. They first played the Cavern on March 21, 1961, for £5 and eventually became the house band as the result of an offer from Bob Wooler, the Cavern's resident disc-jockey. Crowds would gather and queue up along Mathew Street for the lunchtime sessions and during their breaks, the Beatles would escape down the street to the pub called Grapes for their pints of lager, as the Cavern did not sell alcohol.

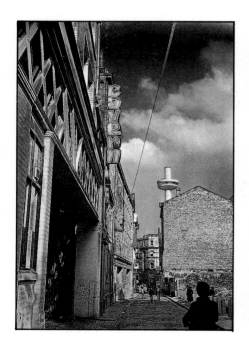

Cavern Club
(continued)

A curious, important and conspicuous visitor to one of these Cavern gigs was Brian Epstein, who first encounterered the Beatles on November 9, 1961 and soon offered to become their manager (see NEMS, *Liverpool*). Also the club's bouncer, Mal Evans, was later to become the Beatles' road manager and one of the chosen few within the private privileged circle.

As the Beatles became famous, the Cavern became known as "the home of the Merseybeat." Other groups such as Gerry and the Pacemakers added to the club's reputation as a showcase of Liverpool's musical talent.

On October 13, 1962, Granada Television filmed the Beatles perfor-

Cars now park where the Cavern Club once stood (left). A souvenir mug from the home of the Mersey sound (above).

ming live at the Cavern. Singing *Some Other Guy*, this visual performance is most likely the earliest recorded moving image of the band in existence. On August 3, 1963, the Beatles played the Cavern for the last time. This time for the sum of £300.

You might say that they paved paradise, as the Cavern Club was torn down in June of 1973 to make way for a subway ventilation shaft. A parking lot now replaces the dark basement cellar where the Beatles performed 294 times. ■

The Cavern Mecca
Beatles' Museum
and Information Centre
18 Mathew Street

The Cavern Mecca is completely dedicated to Liverpool's most famous sons, The Beatles. Here you will find a scene reminiscent of the sixties—a mock Cavern Club interior, complete with stage and housing original memorabilia of the era. The Museum also houses four eight–foot high replica heads of the Fab Four (see above) which were originally designed for the New Cavern Club—across the street from where the original one was torn down. The Centre also has a small coffee-bar, seats around a real fire to sit and talk to other fans and a souvenir counter selling an abundance of Beatles keepsakes. The Cavern Mecca is run by fans (organized by Liz and Jim Hughes whose Magical Mystery Store is incorporated within the Cavern Mecca) and is financially supported by fans through an annual membership. The Cavern Mecca is the closest thing to an offical Liverpool Beatles' tourist centre. True Beatles fans have put together this Museum and meeting place—a site long overdue—that hopefully someday will be supported by the Liverpool City officials. ■

Ringo's sentimental journey: Admiral Grove is the street on the right.

Empress Pub
High Park Street

When Ringo recorded his first solo album in late 1969, not only did he return to the popular standards of an earlier era, he also packaged his production using a photograph of an important monument from his own childhood neighborhood.

The Empress Pub, on the front

cover of *Sentimental Journey*, is located just around the corner from Ringo's Madryn Street birthplace, and another block from his childhood home on Admiral Grove. ■

Frank Hessy's Music Store
62 Stanley Street

Though the Beatles obviously had talent, someone had to supply their instruments. In Liverpool, this someone was Frank Hessy. His music store in the city's center, Whitechapel, carried a variety of instruments and sup-plied most of the young Merseyside bands in the early sixties.

Even John Lennon's Aunt Mimi took him to Hessy's to buy him his first guitar, a steel-stringed Spanish model. And it only cost her £17. Probably one of the greatest in-vestments of our time. ■

Lime Street

Maggie Mae is an old traditional drinking song that tells a sad and sor-did tale of one of Liverpool's loving ladies of the night.

Lime Street
(continued)

Originally the song was one of the dozens of throwaway scraps recorded by the Beatles in 1969. The recording was later salvaged by producer Phil Spector, who discovered it while sifting through the mounds of recorded recitals in an attempt to compile one more Beatles album.

Until it was cleaned up a few years ago, Lime Street attracted at one time many of these passionate pretties. These ladies walked the streets near Liverpool's train station and around the grand Empire Theater offering their services for the right price.

*Oh, dirty Maggie Mae they have
    taken her away
And she'll never walk down Lime
    Street anymore.
Oh, the judge he guilty found her
Of robbing the homeward bounder,
That dirty, no good robbin'
    Maggie Mae.
It's the part of Liverpool she
    returned me to,
Two pound ten a week, that was
    my pay.* ■

The Empire Theater, Lime Street.

North End Music Store-NEMS
12/13 Whitechapel Street

Legend has it that on October 28, 1961, a boy named Raymond Jones strolled into NEMS and requested a record called *My Bonnie* by a group called the Beatles. Brian Epstein, the shop's manager, knew nothing of the group or this newly released recording, but he decided to search out this band of young lads and explore the talents they possessed.

Epstein didn't have to go far. Ninety-eight steps away, around the corner from NEMS, lay the Cavern Club (see Cavern Club, *Liverpool*). There he observed first-hand this musical band of Liverpool locals in black leather coats and tight-fitting trousers. A partnership soon formed which later grew into the historical story of international fame and fortune familiar to us all.

NEMS originally began years earlier as I. Epstein and Sons at the corner of Walton and Royal Roads. Brian's grandfather, Isaac, opened the store which originally sold only furniture. Demonstrating great foresight he subsequently bought North End Road Music Store, located right next door, expanding into radios and record players.

In 1958 the Epstein family opened a second shop in central Liverpool and called the store NEMS after the North End Music Store, which they had incorporated a few years earlier. In 1959 they opened the newest NEMS in Liverpool's Whitechapel district. This was the largest of the family-owned stores. The record department, under Brian's direction, became one of the largest record retailers in Northern England.

The store's offices were on the fourth floor above the record shop. Brian ran his management company from this office and it was here that the Beatles signed their first official contract with Brian. This office at NEMS also witnessed the dismissal of Pete Best from the band. ■

Penny Lane

In February 1967, the Beatles released-their first concept single. It was *Penny Lane* along with *Strawberry Fields Forever*, a double A-sided audio postcard of their childhood neighborhoods. Quiet Penny Lane was transformed into grooves on a record that made it much more than just a quaint little street.

Penny Lane actually refers to the shopping district that revolves around the bus shelter in the middle of the roundabout at Penny Lane and Smithdown Roads. John's Newcastle home is located nearby and as children, it's possible that George and John crossed paths as they waited for the school bus at the roundabout.

To visit the actual street is to see Paul's song come alive. Beneath the blue suburban skies you see the barber shop and the Liverpool Midland Bank surrounding the shelter where one hopes for fish and finger pies. The green buses pass by with their Penny Lane signs stating destination. And if you search for street signs, you'll notice they are gone. Probably because the city got tired of replacing the signs "borrowed" by adoring fans. ∎

The sites of Penny Lane; the Barber shop and the shelter in the middle of the roundabout (opposite). The blue suburban skies with the bank on the right (below).

Penny Lane

*Penny Lane: There is a barber
  showing photographs
Of every head he's had the
  pleasure to know.
And all the people that come and go
Stop and say hello.
On the corner is a banker with a
  motorcar.
The little children laugh at him
  behind his back.
And the banker never wears a mac
In the pouring rain, very strange.
Penny Lane is in my ears and
  in my eyes,
There beneath the blue suburban
  skies
I sit, and meanwhile back
In Penny Lane: There is a fireman
  with an hourglass.
And in his pocket is a portrait
  of the Queen.
He likes to keep his fire engine
  clean,
It's a clean machine.
Penny Lane is in my ears and
  in my eyes
Full of fish and finger pies in
  summer meanwhile back
Behind the shelter in the middle
  of the round-about*

*A pretty nurse is selling poppies
  from a tray.
And though she feels as if she's
  in a play she is anyway.
Penny Lane: The barber shaves
  another customer.
We see the banker sitting, waiting
  for a trim.
And the fireman rushes in
From the pouring rain, very strange.*

*Penny Lane is in my ears and
  in my eyes,
There beneath the blue suburban
  skies
I sit, and meanwhile back
Penny Lane is in my ears and
  in my eyes,
There beneath the blue suburban
  skies...Penny Lane.* ∎

Strawberry Field
Beaconsfield Road

Nothing is real. Nothing to get hung about. Strawberry Fields. Forever. A pink misty image of a cello fantasy from an idealized childhood memory. Let me take you down.

John Lennon's song is one of his most memorable. It is a technical and artistic masterwork, pieced together by George Martin's skills and John Lennon's hallucinogenic imagination. It remains one of the Beatles' milestones–a pivoting point between *Revolver* and *Sgt. Pepper*, touring and the studio.

As *Strawberry Fields* stirs the imagination, blending sight with mind, your first glance at the gates is all you need to begin to feel that you finally have made it to that neighborhood where John Lennon grew up.

Nearby to John's Menlove address

stands this children's orphanage called Strawberry Field. As a kid, John would visit the orphanage when garden shows were presented in its beautiful setting off Beaconsfield Road, a long, narrow, tree-lined lane that adds to the ambience of what you might perceive from the song itself.

Since the old castle-like building was torn down a few years ago and replaced with a newer structure of little interest, only the green, moss-covered, cement gates with their strawberry ironwork continue to supply any magical moments of the vision of John's song. *Cranberry Sauce.* ∎

The old victorian building of the Strawberry Field orphanage, now torn down (above).

Strawberry Fields Forever

Let me take you down
'Cause I'm going to Strawberry
  Fields.
Nothing is real
And nothing to get hung about.
Strawberry Fields Forever.
Living is easy with eyes closed,
Misunderstanding all you see.
It's getting hard to be someone
But it all works out,
It doesn't matter much to me.
Let me take you down
'Cause I'm going to Strawberry
  Fields.
Nothing is real,
And nothing to get hung about.
Strawberry Fields Forever.
No one I think is in my tree
I mean it must be high or low.
That is, you know you can't tune in
But it's all right.
That is, I think it's not too bad.
Let me take you down
'Cause I'm going to Strawberry
  Fields.
Nothing is real,
And nothing to get hung about.
Strawberry Fields Forever.
Always know, sometimes think
  it's me.
But you know when it's a dream.
I think I know I mean a Yes,
But it's all wrong,

That is, I think I disagree.
Let me take you down
'Cause I'm going to Strawberry
  Fields.

Nothing is real,
And nothing to get hung about.
Strawberry Fields Forever.
Strawberry Fields Forever. ■

St. Peter's Church
Church Road, Woolton

John Lennon was the undisputed leader of the Quarrymen, an ever-changing assemblage of high school friends, who somehow managed to produce a sound slightly akin to skiffle rock and roll. John was the best musician in the band, as he reproduced the banjo chords taught to him by his mother Julia on his guitar.

On the afternoon of July 6, 1957, the Quarrymen played a fete at St. Peter's Parrish Church in the Woolton district of Liverpool. Ivan Vaughn, a close mate of John's and a sometimes member of the Quarrymen, invited his friend Paul McCartney along. Paul, at this time, was already somewhat of an accomplished musician.

After the gig, Paul whipped out a guitar and ripped through a version of Eddie Cochran's *Twenty Flight Rock*, concluding with a few of his now-legendary, Little Richard howls. John was impressed. He had met his equal.

Soon after their first meeting, John and Paul began getting together after school. Paul taught John the proper guitar chords along with some of his original tunes. John's imagination was sparked and soon, Woolton Parrish Church became the birthplace of the world's most popular musical partnership. ∎

The social hall at St. Peter's where the Quarrymen performed and John and Paul met (left).

Ye Cracke Pub
Rice Street

Ye Cracke is just around the corner from the Liverpool Art Institute. Today the bright red paint peels from the walls of the semi-secluded rooms. A games board stands out from the wall which is decorated with murals depicting the greatest hits of Napoleon's wars.

Ye Cracke was an integral part of the small developing Liverpool art scene during the late fifties and early sixties. John, Paul and George would often cut school to visit the lively pub. One instructor from the Art Institute even held classes at the pub, believing that the ambience instilled a creative spontaneity. In early 1959, John first met Stuart Sutcliffe at Ye Cracke. Their first conversation laid the foundation for their friendship as each appreciated the other's creative abilities. ∎

Friar Park, Henley-On-Thames

Daytripping

Outside of London and Liverpool   country Inns   castles
towns and villages   ageless Universities   Oxford
Cambridge   winding roads   roundabouts   petrol
holidays by the sea   tea and scones at four   traffic in
the wrong direction   trains on schedule   boat trains to
the Continent   Amsterdam   Hamburg   Paris   Vienna
foreign languages and currency   the Ballad of John and Yoko.

Daytripping

The Ballad of John and Yoko

Standing in the dock at
  Southampton,
Trying to get to Holland or France.
The man in the mac said you've got
  to go back.
You know they didn't even give us
  a chance.

Driving around Southampton in Southern England, you'll discover large painted letters across the roads spelling out D-O-C-K-S. Huge white arrows direct the way towards England's main port for ocean-bound passenger ships.

It was time for an event. March 15, 1969, John and Yoko stood at the Thoresen Passenger Terminal at Southampton waiting to board a France-bound channel ferry. Marriage was on their minds, but passport problems prevented them from boarding.

Finally made the plane into Paris,
Honeymooning down by the Seine.
Peter Brown called to say, you can
  make it ok,
You can get married in Gilbraltar
  near Spain.

Unthwarted in their efforts to make front page news, John and Yoko, along with their assistant Peter Brown, rented a private jet and flew into Paris early the next morning. They checked into the Plaza Athenee

Hotel on the Champs Elysees, and relaxed in the French capital for a few days.

On March 20, they flew to Gilbraltar, at the mouth of the Mediterranean near Spain: "A quiet, British and friendly place." They were married at the Registrar's Office by Cecil Joseph Wheeler. This made the front pages!

Drove from Paris to the Amsterdam
*   Hilton,*
Talking in our beds for a week.
The newspapers said, say what're
*   you doing in bed,*
I said we're only trying to get us
*   some peace.*

John and Yoko display their marriage certificate in front of the Rock of Gibraltar (opposite). The Amsterdam Hilton at 138 Apollolaan (left) and the Docks at Southampton (below).

The Ballad of John & Yoko
(continued)

For seven days in March, room 902 of the Amsterdam Hilton saw more activity than the cocktail lounge downstairs. Up to forty people at a time crowded into the suite, contributing to John and Yoko's Bed-In demonstration against all wars and promoting world peace.

Journalists, photographers, celebrities and friends congregated for ten hours each day inside the crowded cubicle, spreading the word through their songs and stories, hoping that the leaders of the world would stay in bed instead.

On December 14, 1980, during the ten minute silent vigil held for John Lennon, the Amsterdam Hilton, in a touching and emotional gesture, blacked out all the lights throughout the Hotel, except for room 902, which stood out in the black of night. Thousands stood outside, clutching burning candles, remembering the peace movement that occurred here eleven years earlier.

Made a lightning trip to Vienna,
Eating chocolate cake in a bag.
The newspapers said, she's gone to his head,
They look just like two gurus in drag.

With the Bed-In completed, John and Yoko jetted to Vienna, Austria. They held a press conference at the Sacher Hotel to promote their film, *Rape: Film #6*, scheduled to be shown that night on Austrian television. Just to tease and torment the press, they presided over the entire press conference enclosed in large black bags. From Bedism to Bagism.

With all this "silliness," the world press unleashed a deluge of attacks against the two crusaders, missing their point completely.

Christ you know it ain't easy,
You know how hard it can be.
The way things are going,
They're going to crucify me. ∎

Bangor, Wales

On August 24, during 1967's summer of love, the Beatles attended a seminar at London's Hilton Hotel, hosted by the Old Master himself: Maharishi Mahesh Yogi. After a private meeting with the bearded teller of wisdom, the Beatles were invited to a ten-day conference at the University College in Bangor, North Wales.

The kings of popular music left Paddington train station bound for Wales the next day. Accompanied by Pattie Harrison, Jane Asher, Mick Jagger and Marianne Faithfull, they began their journey to discover life's real meaning (Cynthia Lennon missed the train, but joined up with the group later).

Although the sessions were intended to be an exploration of innerpeace, the experience was cut short on August 27, when the news of Brian Epstein's death tainted the holy encounter. With spiritual guidance from "Sexy Sadie," the Beatles returned to London to face reality once again. ■

The Beatles with their Guru arrive at Bangor, Wales (above). George at his Fair-Mile Estate by the pool with John's artwork (left).

Fair-Mile Estate
Claremont Drive, Esher

In July of 1964, George purchased this house—his first after reaching stardom. Psychedelic paisley murals graced the outside walls of the one-story bungalow and a cartoon originally drawn by John was reproduced in mosaic tiles on a wall near the swimming pool. George lived at Fair-Mile until 1969, when he moved to Henley-on-Thames, and into Friar Park. ■

Friar Park

Paradise Road, Henley-on-Thames

Friar Park is a home worthy of a Beatle. In your dreams, you couldn't imagine a more beautiful estate. Friar Park was built in the 1870s by the eccentric Sir Francis Crisp. It consists of forty acres of pure gothic whimsy. The orange stones held together by grey-white mortar blend in with the lush evergreen gardens. The lofty towers and spirals of the main house are surrounded by fields, hedges,

lakes and caves. Even the guest cottages can be considered mansions in their own right.

In February of 1969, George acquired Friar Park from a bankrupt Catholic convent that had planned to destroy the building. Promptly, George found himself unemployed, as his band disintegrated. Lacking anything constructive to fill his hours, he became a gardener, spending hour after hour restoring the grounds to their original botanical splendor.

This "Crackerbox Palace" became the focus of George's creative thoughts. He constructed a recording studio within the walls of the main house, calling it *Friar Park Studios— Henley-on-Thames* or FPSHOT. Along with his records, a number of promotional films were conceived and produced on the grounds. ■

One of the three guest houses on the forty acre estate (opposite). The "Lodge," George's modest little home (top). Discarding the material world: Beatle garbage cans (bottom right). The Row Bardge Pub, just down the road from Frair Park's main gates. One of George's favorite (bottom left).

Helter Skelter
Dreamland Park, Margate

Along the southeast coast of England, in the resort town of Margate, stands Dreamland—the perfect name for the amusement park that the Beatles chose to look to for inspiration for one of their most tempestuous songs: *Helter Skelter* (the original recording was a twenty-five minute explosion that was drastically edited before its release).

It is here at Dreamland that you can find the huge slide known as HELTER SKELTER. Paul's lyrics perfectly describe the long ride down the slippery, glossy surface.

When I get to the bottom I go back
*   to the top of the slide,*
Where I stop and I turn and I go
*   for a ride,*
Till I get to the bottom and I see
*   you again.*   ■

The Helter Skelter slide (left) and the Beatles by the beach at Margate (above).

Kenwood

Cavendish Road, Weybridge

Towards the end of 1964, the Beatles were already an institution, having showered the world with a flood of gold records, a hit movie and a mountain of memorabilia. They had realized the dream of their working class peers—they had lots of money in the bank.

The Beatles had lived in a variety of rented flats (see Beatles Flats, *London*). John Lennon, the "married Beatle" was the first to conform to the traditional pattern by buying a house and attempting to settle down with his family. A modest tudor mansion located in London's "stockbroker belt" in Weybridge was chosen as the Lennons' first house. The estate is called Kenwood. It was acquired for ±40,000 in 1964 and the family lived here until 1968, when John and Cynthia separated. ∎

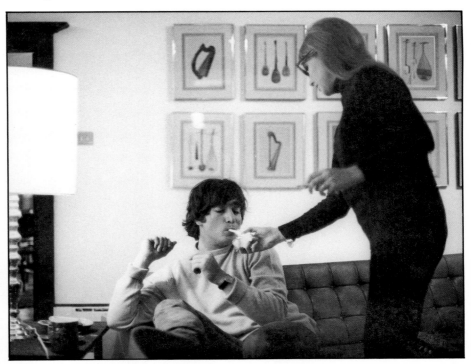

John and Cynthia: family life number one (above). A really big shoe (left) on the grounds at Kenwood.

Lady Mitchell Hall

Cambridge University

Cambridge, without a doubt, is one of the world's most prestigious universities. Massive stone halls topped with gothic towers are entwined by narrow cobblestone alleys that are crowded with bright young scholars on bicycles and aging professors carrying the history of the ages.

In a remote section of the campus

stands Lady Mitchell Hall, a rather uninteresting lecture hall of modern design.

On March 2, 1969, John and Yoko performed their first breach of the peace. It was a mini-show of shows, an artistic endeavor shockingly witnessed by the audience. During this "free jazz festival" (a pseudonym for noise, outside the realm of music), Yoko sang and John produced feedback on his electric guitar. Together they executed a concert that molded together pop and avant-garde music, a program that in future times would take its place alongside the works of Harry Partch, John Cage and Brian Eno, to name but a few.

An important note about this interesting production is that it was the first solo-Beatle performance. The sounds produced that night were subsequently released for public consumption on Side One of *Unfinished Music #2—Life with the Lions* on Zapple Records (see Queen Charlotte's Hospital, *London*). ∎

Stonehenge
Salisbury Plain

Approximately thirty miles southwest of London, on an isolated plain near the town of Salisbury, stand the ruins of an ancient temple brought to Earth by aliens from some far away galaxy. We refer to it as Stonehenge. There are many other theories about the origin of Stonehenge but very little substantiated proof. It dates back

Stonehenge

(continued)

to a prehistoric period, long before any written records were made.

Perhaps visiting aliens were simply Beatles fans wishing to observe the filming of a sequence from *Help!* but were thousands of years too early.

A few miles to the north of these ruins is an outpost of Her Majesty's Royal Army, making the Salisbury Plain an ideal site for a recording session when you are being pursued by Clang, the High Priest of the dreaded Kaili, seen in the film *Help!*

Any other facts about this amazing historical site can be found in hundreds of other books and articles. ■

Sunny Heights

St. George's Road, Weybridge

Ringo purchased his Sunny Heights residence in 1965 for £35,000 and lived here with his first wife, Maureen, until 1968. It is located just outside London in Weybridge and is quite close to John's Kenwood estate. With two Beatles living so close to each other, it was once rumored that Brian Epstein had the dream of an entire Beatles village. ■

Ringo, Maureen, records and bongos.

Tittenhurst Park
London Road, Ascot

This large, white, 18th-century Georgian manor was John and Yoko's home from 1969 through 1972 when they left England and moved to New York. They purchased the home, set amidst some eighty acres, for £150,000.

John had an eight-track recording studio built inside his new home, allowing him to record his *Imagine* LP in the comfort of his own surroundings. Tittenhurst Park provided the background for the collaborative *Imagine* film that combined John's album with Yoko's *Fly* LP for the soundtrack.

The Beatles' last official photo session was held on the wild, overgrown grounds. Two of these photos appear on the *Hey Jude* album.

Ringo moved into Tittenhurst Park when John and Yoko moved to New York and eventually purchased the estate from the Ono-Lennons. ∎

John and Yoko: family life number two.
Tittenhurst Park.

West Malling Airfield

A 228 Highway, West Malling, Kent County

Nestled away in the English countryside south of London is the West Malling Airfield. All that is visible amidst the grass and bushes that skirt the abandoned runways are massive cement slabs, reaching upward out of the nothingness. All is quiet except for the sound of birds and the scraping of wind against the surrounding trees.

Suddenly you turn around, only to be greeted by the music from a band of cellos and then a set of drums that crash against the soft daylight. From out of nowhere, four animal-like creatures appear. They are half-man and half-beastly musician. One plays the

guitar, another a bass, a third pounds on the drums and the last is perched behind a large, white grand piano. As they perform, a line of pretty policemen form a perfect row, and mutated eggmen surround these storybook creatures.

Has the world gone mad? Or have the Beatles just released another new record? Yes friends, it is *I Am the Walrus* and the scene is from *Magical Mystery Tour*. It is here at West Malling that much of the adventure was filmed. As an alternative to the overbooked Shepperton Film Studios, abandoned airplane hangars were used as a studio for interior shots. The West Malling Airfield was an ideal retreat, lending itself perfectly to the production of this madcap, Felliniesque episode. ∎

HAMBURG CLUBS (Germany)

Hamburg is a typical German industrial city, having been reconstructed heavily after the second World War with spacious concrete buildings and flourishing green parks. However, stories of this seaport city are full of sin and sleaze. One expects to be constantly surrounded by intense wickedness. This side of Hamburg can be found in a seemingly legal, well-defined area known as the Reeperbahn, in the St. Pauli district of the city. Empty streets in the daytime awaken

at night. Neon tubes buzz with erotic excitement. Silhouettes of women, animals, mysterious German words and beer brands light up the dark streets that clamour with the throbbing tension of vice. Barkers at every doorway demand your attention as they try to lure you into their pleasure palaces.

On certain sidestreets, young girls stand alongside the buildings every ten feet or so, grabbing hold of men's arms as if heading towards their Senior Proms. The increased popularity and commercialization of Hamburg's sexual kingdom has changed somewhat since the Beatles worked at the Reeperbahn's clubs more than twenty years ago. One can imagine them, in their late teens, away from

Hamburg Clubs
(continued)

home for the first time in a city that offers and consumes what this one does.

In early 1960 the Liverpool beat scene flourished with modest excitement. Simultaneously in Hamburg, a similar scene of entertainment was developing. Both cities had clubs and bars where beat bands would perform and hang out.

Two entrepreneurs, both in their respective cities, crossed paths by accident, paving the way for the eventual migration of Liverpool groups to Hamburg. Allan Williams in Liverpool owned the Jacaranda and the Blue Angel clubs. Bruno Koschmider ran the Kaiserkeller and the Indra in Hamburg. The two came into contact with each other when a steel drum band playing in the basement of the Jacaranda packed up and left for Koschmider's Kaiserkeller. Williams, who was managing and booking a number of Liverpool bands, had an idea to develop a similar beat scene in Hamburg by sending over bands to play in the German clubs.

Arrangements were made to have Liverpool's Derry and the Seniors play the Kaiserkeller. The band was a hit and Koschmider wanted more bands. Rory Storm and the Hurricanes were chosen, but declined because of other bookings. Gerry and the Pacemakers, next on the list, didn't want to leave England. The third-choice Beatles accepted the invitation. ∎

Indra Club

34 Grosse Freiheit

Allan Williams, his wife Beryl and their friend, chauffeur and sidekick Lord Woodbine, a West Indian who ran a couple of the Liverpool clubs, packed the Beatles into a van and drove them via Newhaven and the Hoek Van Holland to Hamburg. They were given lodging behind the screen of an old movie house on Grosse Freiheit, and were immediately put to work at the Indra Club. Their first show was on August 17, 1960.

The Indra was Koschmider's second club, a small hole in the wall lacking the excitement of his larger Kaiserkeller. Having witnessed the fervor generated by Derry and the

Indra Club
(continued)

Seniors at the Kaiserkeller, the reality of the small, almost empty Indra was a disappointment to the Beatles.

Their prime purpose of employment was not, at this point, to advance this fine form of music, but rather to attract beer buying customers, probably advancing the fine form of alcoholism.

The Beatles were encouraged to make lots of noise, jump around and attract a lot of attention. They had to put on a show, or *Mak Show*, as it sounded from the thick German accents. This gave the Beatles, and especially John, a license for lunacy. They were on stage some six to eight hours each night, playing any song they could think of, saying anything that came to mind and doing anything to attract paying customers. Amphetamines and "prellys" fueled their adrenaline. Guzzled beers quenched their dry mouths. People came and crowds began to form, filling up the small club.

Soon, the lady living upstairs from the club complained about the noise level. The Indra was shut down, and the Beatles were moved to the larger and more illustrious Kaiserkeller. ∎

Kaiserkeller

36 Grosse Freiheit

Pills, beer and sex helped settle the Beatles into the Kaiserkeller on a nightly basis. Rory Storm's band had replaced Derry and the Seniors, sharing the bill with the Beatles. John, Paul and George now became close friends with Ringo, who was drumming with Rory Storm. They shared wild times together while Pete Best dedicated himself to a slightly more normal existence.

Klaus Voorman wandered into the Kaiserkeller one night. Voorman was one of the intellectual, existentialist, artist-types, who was intrigued and attracted by the visual style presented by the Beatles. (Klaus Voorman would later draw the cover for the Beatles' *Revolver* album.) He began bringing friends to see the Beatles. One was Astrid Kirschner, who probably is the single most important person who should be credited for inventing the Beatles' hairstyle. For it was Astrid who, after falling in love with

The Kaiserkeller today.

Kaiserkeller
(continued)

Stuart Sutcliffe, changed his hair-style into what would be known as the Beatle-haircut. She supposedly said to Stuart, "Well Stu, why don't we cut your hair, comb it down in front, and invent the Beatle haircut?"

A comradery developed between the German art crowd and many of the British beat groups, who were outsiders, usually mingling amongst themselves. They were bands of musical soldiers that up to this point hadn't blended in socially. ■

Top Ten Club
136 Reeperbahn

In November of 1960, the Top Ten Club opened up on the Reeperbahn. It was a new and larger club than the Kaiserkeller, offering direct competition. Its first act was Tony Sheridan, an English, Elvis-like singer from Liverpool, who became a regular at the club. Lured by offers of higher wages and glamour everyone, including the waiters, bouncers and bands, began defecting to the newest of the hot-spots: the Top Ten. Of course, the Beatles were no different.

Bruno Koschmider chose to notice a previously ignored illegality when the Beatles left the Kaiserkeller to play the Top Ten. Not only did the

Stuart Sutcliffe and John Lennon at the Top Ten Club, 1961 (below).

Beatles not have the proper work permits, but George was also under the legal age. George was deported first. Next, Paul and Pete were arrested and accused of setting fire to their behind-the-screen lodgings. Finally Stuart flew home while John carried all the equipment back to Liverpool by train (see Litherland Town Hall, *Liverpool*).

The Beatles returned to Hamburg and the Top Ten in April, 1961. This time they had proper work permits and were a somewhat more polished group. They arrived by train and soon slipped back into their old Hamburg habits.

Stuart was becoming inspired by both the Hamburg art scene and Astrid, who was an artist and photog-

Top Ten Club
(continued)

rapher herself. He soon retired from the Beatles and enrolled in Hamburg's State Art College, passing down his role as bass player to Paul.

The Beatles carried on at the Top Ten, sharing the bill with Tony Sheridan. Sheridan had a recording contract with Polydor Records and used the Beatles as his backing band under the name of the Beat Brothers. On the record are *My Bonnie Lies Over the Ocean* and *When the Saints Go Marching In,* which became the released single (and requested by Raymond Jones in Brian Epstein's record shop). They also recorded an original Lennon and Harrison composition called *Cry for a Shadow* and a version of *Ain't She Sweet* sung by John.

They were paid a flat fee for the session of 300 DM, but have been repaid many times over for that wonderful record (see NEMS, *Liverpool*). ∎

Star Club

39 Grosse Freiheit

By spring 1962, the Beatles were legends of sorts in two seaports, but nowhere else. Their career was stalemated as they ping-ponged between Liverpool and Hamburg. On April 13, 1962 they were top of the bill at the newest of the St. Pauli clubs: The Star Club. The biggest and best of them all. A huge palace converted from an old cinema, completely dwarfing the Kaiserkeller and the Top Ten clubs.

This was the Beatles' third trip to Hamburg. They arrived by plane, this time under the guidance of a real manager, Brian Epstein. Their arrival, however, was greeted by the sad news that Stuart Sutcliffe had died of a brain hemorrhage two days earlier.

During their run at the Star Club, the Beatles received the now famous cable from Brian Epstein in England. He had secured them an audition with George Martin at Parlaphone Records (see Abbey Road Studios and HMV, *London*).

When they returned once again to the Star Club on December 18, 1962, they were under contract with Parlaphone and Ringo Starr had replaced

The back cover of the Beatles Live at the Star Club album, showing the front entrance of the club (left). The Star Club in its new incarnation (right).

Star Club
(continued)

Pete Best. Their final Reeperbahn appearance was on New Year's Eve in 1962, at the Star Club.

Like the Cavern Club, the Star Club became a world-famous mecca for rock-and-roll talent, featuring the Searchers, Little Richard, Cream, Jimi Hendrix and many more. A Star Club record label was formed, and the original club eventually closed its doors in 1969 and later opened in another location in the early seventies with Tony Sheridan, once again, on opening night. Ringo and George were in the audience that night. ∎

The New Star Club today at 43 Alter Steinweg.

British Sailors' Society
Johannis Bollwerk

What would you do if you were a band member living in a foreign country without money and lots of empty daytime hours? Leave the answer to the adventurous Beatles. Adjacent to Hamburg's harbor, within walking distance of the Reeperbahn is the home of the British Sailors' Society.

The Beatles discovered this home away from home in 1960 and it soon became one of their early Hamburg haunts. The Beatles knew of the Society's Liverpool branch and were quick to adopt the Hamburg version as their meeting and eating place.

It was the closest they could find to Liverpool's lunch and breakfast style, usually having cornflakes and milk. Dedicated to making sailors away from home feel comfortable, the Sailors' Society took in this group of musicians, as they too were outbound seamen of sorts, hungry, lonely and, most importantly, away from home. ∎

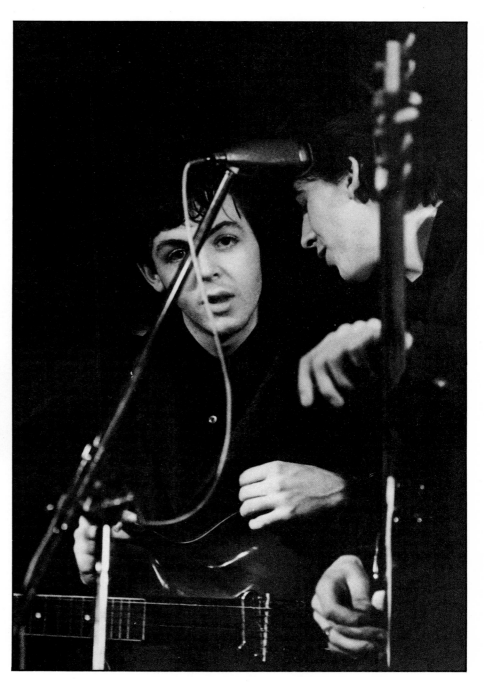

Photographic Credits

Bibliography

Castleman, Harry and Podrazik, Wally. *All Together Now*. Ann Arbor: Pierian Press, 1975.

Castleman, Harry and Podrazik, Wally. *The Beatles Again*. Ann Arbor: Pierian Press, 1977.

Davies, Hunter. *The Beatles, The Authorized Biography*. New York: McGraw-Hill, 1968.

Di Franco, J. Phillip. *A Hard Day's Night*. New York: Chelsea House, 1977.

DiLello, Richard. *The Longest Cocktail Party*. New York: Playboy Press, 1972.

Fawcett, Anthoney. *John Lennon: One Day at a Time*. New York: Grove Press, 1976.

Friede, Goldie and Titone, Robin and Weiner, Sue. *The Beatles A to Z*, New York: Methuen, 1980.

Harrison, George. *I Me Mine*. Guildford: Genesis Publications, 1980.

Harry, Bill. *Mersey Beat: The Beginnings of the Beatles*. London: Omnibus Press, 1977.

Jackson, Michael. *Exploring England*. New York: Mayflower Books, 1979.

Nicholson, Robert. *Nicholson's London Guide*. London: Nicholson Publications, 1980.

Norman, Philip. *Shout! The Beatles in their Generation*. New York: Fireside Books, 1981.

Schaffner, Nicholas. *The Beatles Forever*. Harrisburg: Cameron, 1977.

Schultheiss, Tom. *A Day In the Life*. Ann Arbor: Pierian Press, 1980.

Webster. *Webster's Dictionary of the English Language Unabridged Encyclopedic Edition*. New York: Publishers International Press, 1977.

Williams, Allan and Marshall, William. *The Man Who Gave the Beatles Away*. New York: Macmillian, 1975.

The following telephone directories: *London Postal Area—Volumes A–Z. London Central Yellow Pages. Mersey Yellow Pages*. 1979–1981.

Thank U Very Much

Jenny Abbe
Margaret Bacon
Stan and Betty Bacon
David Barich
Cavern Mecca (Jim and Liz)
Core Group
Dai Nippon (Toshihiko Miyazaki
  and Mikio Shinohara)
Philip Emerick
Katherine Feinstein
Brooks Frank
Louis Freedman
Bennett "Superfly" Friedman
Jerry Gardner
Steve Garland
Annette Goldberg
James Grady
Kathy Greenstone
Jay Hansen
Bill Henkin
Karen Hill
Debi Horen
Prudy and George Kohler

Jimmy Lyford
Madame Tussaud's
Paul and Regina Maslov
Elliot and Sandra Mazer
Vernon McNemar
Hale Milgrim
Harold Montgomery
Nancy Newhouse
Denise Nichols
Philip Norman
Cliff Palefsky
Don Patterson
Brenn Lea Pearson
Ann Peterson
Nicholas Schaffner
Madeleine Schatz
Karen Schein
Wendy Schwartz
Mollie Shragge
Larry and Debbie Weinberg
Allan and Beryl Williams
Eric Wolf
Cliff Yamasaki

The Authors: *Somewhere in England.*

Norman Maslov (left) was born and currently lives in San Francisco. He has a degree in Broadcast Communication Arts from San Francisco State University, and has written letters to Rolling Stone Magazine (only one was published). He missed the last Beatles' concert at Candlestick Park in 1966 because he had a drum lesson that night. He no longer plays the drums.

David Bacon (right) was born sometime ago in Yokosuka, Japan. Several years later he graduated from San Francisco State University with a degree in Film. He is the Producer/Director of the award winning film, *Confessions of a Beatlemaniac*, and was the second place winner of the Beatle-brain quiz in Sheffield, England in 1980.

The Designer: *Somewhere.*

Brenn Lea Pearson was also born sometime ago in Geneva, Illinois. She has a degree from the University of Denver which is minorly related to her award-winning graphic design business in San Francisco. Although she never saw the Beatles in concert, she does admit to listening to their music on more than one occasion. She never took drum lessons and certainly never entered a Beatle-brain quiz. So it goes.